D0640949

For current pricing information,
or to learn more about this or any Nextext title,
call us toll-free at **1-800-323-5435**
or visit our web site at www.nextext.com.

WITHDRAWN

A HISTORICAL READER

The
IMMIGRANTS

Compiled by: Ethel Wood, Princeton High School, Princeton, New Jersey.

Cover photograph: An Italian family on the deck of a ferry boat arriving at Ellis Island, New York, in 1905. Photograph by Lewis W. Hine (1874-1940). Courtesy of George Eastman House.

Printed in the United States of America

ISBN 0-618-04818-9

2 3 4 5 6 7 — QKT — 06 05 04 03 02 01

Table of Contents

*Throughout the reader, vocabulary words appear in boldface
type and are footnoted. Specialized or technical words and phrases
appear in lightface type and are footnoted.*

Immigration in Early America

What Is an American?

BY J. HECTOR ST. JOHN DE CRÈVECOEUR

Crèvecoeur, a French officer who became a resident of New York, was a farmer who achieved fame when his Letters from an American Farmer *caught the attention of American political leaders such as Benjamin Franklin. This excerpt from one of his most notable essays reflects the high aspirations of many who immigrated to North America during the eighteenth century. His view of a nation where "individuals of all nations are melted into a new race of men" has influenced American attitudes toward immigration throughout the country's history.*

I wish I could be acquainted with the feelings and thoughts which must agitate the heart and present themselves to the mind of an enlightened Englishman when he first lands on this continent. He must greatly rejoice that he lived at a time to see this fair country discovered and settled; he must necessarily feel a share of national pride when he views the chain of settlements which embellish these extended shores. When he says to himself, "This is the work of my countrymen, who, when convulsed by factions,[1] afflicted by a variety of miseries and wants, restless and impatient, took refuge here. They brought along with them their national genius, to which they principally owe what liberty they enjoy and what substance they possess." Here he sees the industry of his native country displayed in a new manner and traces in their works the embryos[2] of all the arts, sciences, and ingenuity which flourish in Europe. Here he beholds fair cities, substantial villages, extensive fields, an immense country filled with decent houses, good roads, orchards, meadows, and bridges where a hundred years ago all was wild, woody, and uncultivated! What a train of pleasing ideas this fair spectacle must suggest; it is a prospect which must inspire a good citizen with the most heart-felt pleasure. The difficulty consists in the manner of viewing so extensive a scene. He is arrived on a new continent; a modern society offers itself to his contemplation, different from what he had hitherto seen. It is not composed, as in Europe, of great lords who possess everything and of a herd of people who have nothing. Here are no aristocratical families, no courts, no kings, no bishops, no ecclesiastical dominion,[3] no invisible power giving to a few a very visible one, no great manufacturers employing thousands, no great refinements of luxury. The rich and the poor are not so far removed from each other as they are in Europe. Some few towns excepted, we are all tillers of the earth, from Nova Scotia to West Florida. We are a people of cultivators scattered over an immense territory, communicating with each other by means of good roads and navigable rivers, united by the silken bands of mild government, all respecting the laws without dreading their power, because they are **equitable**.[4]

---

[1] convulsed by factions—disrupted by quarreling groups.

[2] embryos—seeds.

[3] ecclesiastical dominion—church authority.

[4] **equitable**—fair.

We are all animated with the spirit of an industry which is unfettered and unrestrained, because each person works for himself. If he travels through our rural districts, he views not the hostile castle and the haughty mansion, contrasted with the clay-built hut and miserable cabin, where cattle and men help to keep each other warm and dwell in meanness, smoke, and **indigence**.[5] A pleasing uniformity of decent competence appears throughout our habitations.

The next wish of this traveler will be to know whence came all these people. They are a mixture of English, Scotch, Irish, French, Dutch, Germans, and Swedes. From this **promiscuous**[6] breed, that race now called Americans has arisen. . . .

In this great American asylum, the poor of Europe have by some means met together, and in consequence of various causes; to what purpose should they ask one another what countrymen they are? Alas, two thirds of them had no country. Can a wretch who wanders about, who works and starves, whose life is a continual scene of sore affliction or pinching **penury**[7]—can that man call England or any other kingdom his country? A country that had no bread for him, whose fields procured him no harvest, who met with nothing but the frowns of the rich, the severity of the laws, with jails and punishments, who owned not a single foot of the extensive surface of this planet? No! Urged by a variety of motives, here they came.

What, then, is the American, this new man? He is neither an European nor the descendant of an European; hence that strange mixture of blood, which you will find in no other country. I could point out to you a family whose grandfather was an Englishman, whose wife was

---

[5] **indigence**—poverty.

[6] **promiscuous**—consisting of different elements, indiscriminately mingled.

[7] **penury**—poverty.

Dutch, whose son married a French woman, and whose present four sons have now four wives of different nations. *He* is an American, who, leaving behind him all his ancient prejudices and manners, receives new ones from the new mode of life he has embraced, the new government he obeys, and the new rank he holds. He becomes an American by being received in the broad lap of our great Alma Mater. Here individuals of all nations are melted into a new race of men, whose labors and **posterity**[8] will one day cause great changes in the world. Americans are the western pilgrims who are carrying along with them that great mass of arts, sciences, vigor, and industry which began long since in the East; they will finish the great circle. The Americans were once scattered all over Europe; here they are incorporated into one of the finest systems of population which has ever appeared, and which will hereafter become distinct by the power of the different climates they inhabit. The American ought therefore to love this country much better than that wherein either he or his forefathers were born. Here the rewards of his industry follow with equal steps the progress of his labor; his labor is founded on the basis of nature, self-interest; can it want a stronger **allurement**?[9] Wives and children, who before in vain demanded of him a morsel of bread, now, fat and frolicsome, gladly help their father to clear those fields whence exuberant crops are to arise to feed and to clothe them all, without any part being claimed, either by a **despotic**[10] prince, a rich abbot, or a mighty lord. Here religion demands but little of him: a small voluntary salary to the minister and gratitude to God; can he refuse these? The American is a new man, who sets upon new principles; he must therefore entertain new ideas and

---

[8] **posterity**—descendants.

[9] **allurement**—appeal.

[10] **despotic**—tyrannical.

form new opinions. From involuntary idleness, servile dependence, penury, and useless labor, he has passed to toils of a very different nature, rewarded by ample subsistence. This is an American.

An European, when he first arrives, seems limited in his intentions, as well as in his views; but he very suddenly alters his scale; two hundred miles formerly appeared a very great distance, it is now but a trifle; he no sooner breathes our air than he forms schemes and embarks in designs he never would have thought of in his own country. There the **plenitude**[11] of society confines many useful ideas and often extinguishes the most **laudable**[12] schemes, which here ripen into maturity. Thus Europeans become Americans.

But how is this accomplished in that crowd of low, indigent people who flock here every year from all parts of Europe? I will tell you; they no sooner arrive than they immediately feel the good effects of that plenty of provisions we possess. . . .

He is encouraged, he has gained friends; he is advised and directed; he feels bold, he purchases some land; he gives all the money he has brought over, as well as what he has earned, and trusts to the God of harvests for the discharge of the rest. His good name procures him credit. He is now possessed of the deed, conveying to him and his posterity the fee simple and absolute property of two hundred acres of land, situated on such a river. What an **epoch**[13] in this man's life! He is become a freeholder, from perhaps a German boor. He is now an American, a Pennsylvanian, an English subject. He is naturalized; his name is enrolled with those of the other citizens of the province. . . . From nothing to start into being; from a servant to the rank of a master; from being the slave of some despotic prince, to become a free man,

---

[11] **plenitude**—fullness, abundance.

[12] **laudable**—praiseworthy.

[13] **epoch**—noteworthy period.

invested with lands to which every municipal blessing is annexed! What a change indeed! It is in consequence of that change that he becomes an American. This great **metamorphosis**[14] has a double effect: it extinguishes all his European prejudices, he forgets that mechanism of subordination, that **servility**[15] of disposition which poverty had taught him; and sometimes he is apt to forget it too much, often passing from one extreme to the other. . . . Ye poor Europeans—ye who sweat and work for the great; ye who are obliged to give so many **sheaves**[16] to the church, so many to your lords, so many to your government, and have hardly any left for yourselves; ye who are held in less estimation than favorite hunters or useless lap-dogs; ye who only breathe the air of nature because it cannot be withholden from you—it is here that ye can conceive the possibility of those feelings I have been describing; it is here the laws of naturalization invite every one to partake of our great labors and felicity, to till unrented, untaxed lands!

---

[14] **metamorphosis**—complete change.

[15] **servility**—behaving like a servant; submissiveness.

[16] **sheaves**—bundles of grain. This is a reference to the way some Biblical passages describe taxes.

QUESTIONS TO CONSIDER

1. What would an "enlightened Englishman" have to be proud of when first seeing America? In what ways does Crèvecoeur see America as superior to European countries?

2. What, in your opinion, is the answer to Crèvecoeur's question: "What, then, is the American, this new man?"

3. How does Crèvecoeur say that the new immigrant is transformed when he or she reaches America?

4. Is Crèvecoeur's description of early American society over idealized? Why or why not?

The Difficulties of Immigration

BY GOTTLIEB MITTELBERGER

In the eighteenth century, thousands of people from the German Rhineland were recruited by "soul traffickers," who received a commission for each victim they convinced to come to Pennsylvania. Gottlieb Mittelberger, a German pastor, crossed the Atlantic about 1750 to investigate reports of ill treatment of these German immigrants both before and during their voyage to America. In his account, he describes the misery of the journey as well as "the sale of human beings" at the end of the voyage. The immigrants became indentured servants, forced to work several years for a new master in exchange for his payment for their passage.

When the ships have weighed anchor for the last time, usually off Cowes in Old England, then both the long sea voyage and misery begin in earnest. For from there the ships often take eight, nine, ten, or twelve weeks sailing to Philadelphia, if the wind is unfavorable. But even given the most favorable winds, the voyage takes seven weeks.

During the journey the ship is full of pitiful signs of distress—smells, fumes, horrors, vomiting, various kinds of sea sickness, fever, dysentery, headaches, heat, constipation, boils, scurvy, cancer, mouth-rot, and similar afflictions, all of them caused by the age and the highly-salted state of the food, especially of the meat, as well as by the very bad and filthy water, which brings about the miserable destruction and death of many. Add to all that shortage of food, hunger, thirst, frost, heat, dampness, fear, misery, **vexation**,[1] and lamentation[2] as well as other troubles. Thus, for example, there are so many lice, especially on the sick people, that they have to be scraped off the bodies. All this misery reaches its climax when in addition to everything else one must also suffer through two to three days and nights of storm, with everyone convinced that the ship with all aboard is bound to sink. In such misery all the people on board pray and cry pitifully together.

In the course of such a storm the sea begins to surge and rage so that the waves often seem to rise up like high mountains, sometimes sweeping over the ship; and one thinks that he is going to sink along with the ship. All the while the ship, tossed by storm and waves, moves constantly from one side to the other, so that nobody aboard can either walk, sit, or lie down and the tightly packed people on their cots, the sick as well as the healthy, are thrown every which way. One can easily imagine that these hardships necessarily affect many people so severely that they cannot survive them.

Among those who are in good health impatience sometimes grows so great and bitter that one person begins to curse the other, or himself and the day of his birth, and people sometimes come close to murdering

[1] **vexation**—distress.

[2] lamentation—cries of grief.

one another. Misery and malice are readily associated, so that people begin to cheat and steal from one another. And then one always blames the other for having undertaken the voyage. Often the children cry out against their parents, husbands against wives and wives against husbands, brothers against their sisters, friends and acquaintances against one another.

But most of all they cry out against the thieves of human beings! Many groan and exclaim: "Oh! If only I were back at home, even lying in my pig-sty!" Or they call out: "Ah, dear God, if I only once again had a piece of good bread or a good fresh drop of water." Many people whimper, sigh, and cry out pitifully for home. Most of them become homesick at the thought that many hundreds of people must necessarily perish, die, and be thrown into the ocean in such misery. . . . In a word, groaning, crying, and lamentation go on aboard day and night; so that even the hearts of the most hardened, hearing all this, begin to bleed.

When at last after the long and difficult voyage the ships finally approach land, when one gets to see the headlands for the sight of which the people on board had longed so passionately, then everyone crawls from below to the deck, in order to look at the land from afar. And people cry for joy, pray, and sing praises and thanks to God. The glimpse of land revives the passengers, especially those who are half-dead of illness. Their spirits, however weak they had become, leap up, triumph, and rejoice within them. Such people are now willing to bear all ills patiently, if only they can disembark[3] soon and step on land. But, alas, alas!

When the ships finally arrive in Philadelphia after the long voyage only those are let off who can pay their sea freight or can give good security. The others, who lack the money to pay, have to remain on board until

---

[3] disembark—get off the ship.

they are purchased and until their purchasers can thus pry them loose from the ship. In this whole process the sick are the worst off, for the healthy are preferred and are more readily paid for. The miserable people who are ill must often still remain at sea and in sight of the city for another two or three weeks—which in many cases means death. Yet many of them, were they able to pay their debts and to leave the ships at once, might escape with their lives.

This is how the commerce in human beings on board ship takes place. Every day Englishmen, Dutchmen, and High Germans come from Philadelphia and other places, some of them very far away, sometimes twenty or thirty or forty hours' journey, and go on board the newly arrived vessel that has brought people from Europe and offers them for sale. From among the healthy they pick out those suitable for the purposes for which they require them. Then they negotiate with them as to the length of the period for which they will go into service in order to pay off their passage, the whole amount of which they generally still owe. When an agreement has been reached, adult persons by written contract bind themselves to serve for three, four, five, or six years, according to their health and age. The very young, between the ages of ten and fifteen, have to serve until they are twenty-one, however.

Many parents in order to pay their fares in this way and get off the ship must barter and sell their children as if they were cattle. Since the fathers and mothers often do not know where or to what masters their children are to be sent, it frequently happens that after leaving the vessel, parents and children do not see each other for years on end, or even for the rest of their lives.

It often happens that whole families—husband, wife, and children—being sold to different purchasers, become separated, especially when they cannot pay any part of the passage money. When either the husband or the wife has died at sea, having come more than halfway, then the surviving spouse must pay not only his or her fare, but must also pay for or serve out the fare of the deceased.

No one in this country can run away from a master who has treated him harshly and get far. For there are regulations and laws that ensure that runaways are certainly and quickly recaptured. Those who arrest or return a fugitive get a good reward. For every day that someone who runs away is absent from his master he must as a punishment do service an extra week, for every week an extra month, and for every month a half year. But if the master does not want to take back the recaptured runaway, he is entitled to sell him to someone else for the period of as many years as he would still have had to serve.

QUESTIONS TO CONSIDER

1. What difficulties did the immigrants endure while crossing the Atlantic?

2. What were some of the causes of their miseries?

3. What problems did immigrants face after their crossing?

The Alien and Sedition Acts

ENACTED BY THE UNITED STATES CONGRESS

Even though early American immigration was generally unrestricted, negative attitudes toward immigrants were present almost from the beginning. Anti-immigrant feelings were magnified by the first two American political parties, with many foreign-born persons preferring the Democratic Republican Party over the Federalists. In 1798, as the nation experienced international tension and faced possible war with France, a Federalist-controlled Congress passed the Alien and Sedition Acts in an attempt to halt their Democratic Republican critics and control potential spying activities. In these acts, signed into law by President John Adams, "aliens"—immigrants—were presumed to be involved in conspiracy and anti-government activities. Neither act was renewed after it expired.

Alien Act

Section I: President's Power to Deport and License Aliens

Be it enacted by the Senate and House of Representatives of the United States of America in

Congress assembled, That it shall be lawful for the President of the United States at any time during the continuance of this act, to order all such **aliens**[1] as he shall judge dangerous to the peace and safety of the United States, or shall have reasonable grounds to suspect are concerned in any treasonable or secret **machinations**[2] against the government thereof, to depart out of the territory of the United States, within such time as shall be expressed in such order, which order shall be served on such alien by delivering him a copy thereof, or leaving the same at his usual abode, and returned to the office of the Secretary of State, by the marshal or other person to whom the same shall be directed. And in case any alien, so ordered to depart, shall be found at large within the United States after the time limited in such order for his departure, and not having obtained a license shall not have conformed thereto, every such alien shall, on conviction thereof, be imprisoned for a term not exceeding three years, and shall never after be admitted to become a citizen of the United States.

Provided always, and be it further enacted, that if any alien so ordered to depart shall prove to the satisfaction of the President, by evidence to be taken before such person or persons as the President shall direct, who are for that purpose hereby authorized to administer oaths, that no injury or danger to the United States will arise from suffering such alien to reside therein, the President may grant a license to such alien to remain within the United States for such time as he shall judge proper, and at such place as he may designate.

And the President may also require of such alien to enter into a bond to the United States, in such penal sum as he may direct, with one or more sufficient **sureties**[3] to the satisfaction of the person authorized by the

---

[1] **aliens**—foreign-born persons.

[2] **machinations**—plots.

[3] **sureties**—bonds.

President to take the same, conditioned for the good behavior of such alien during his residence in the United States, and not violating his license, which license the President may revoke, whenever he shall think proper.

Section 2: President's Power to Deport and Imprison Violators

And be it further enacted, That it shall be lawful for the President of the United States, whenever he may deem it necessary for the public safety, to order to be removed out of the territory thereof, any alien who may or shall be in prison in pursuance of this act; and to cause to be arrested and sent out of the United States such of those aliens as shall have been ordered to depart there from and shall not have obtained a license as aforesaid, in all cases where, in the opinion of the President, the public safety requires a speedy removal.

And if any alien so removed or sent out of the United States by the President shall voluntarily return thereto, unless by permission of the President of the United States, such alien on conviction thereof, shall be imprisoned so long as, in the opinion of the President, the public safety may require.

Section 3: Ship Commander Reports

And be it further enacted, That every master or commander of any ship or vessel which shall come into any port of the United States after the first day of July next, shall immediately on his arrival make report in writing to the collector or other chief officer of the customs of such port, of all aliens, if any, on board his vessel, specifying their names, age, the place of **nativity**,[4] the country from which they shall have come, the nation to which they belong and owe allegiance, their occupation and a description of their persons, as far as he shall be

---

[4] **nativity**—birth.

informed thereof, and on failure, every such master and commander shall forfeit and pay three hundred dollars, for the payment whereof on default of such master or commander, such vessel shall also be holden, and may by such collector or other officer of the customs be detained.

And it shall be the duty of such collector or other officer of the customs, forthwith to transmit to the office of the department of state true copies of all such returns.

Section 4: Courts and U.S. Officers

And be it further enacted, That the circuits and district courts of the United States shall respectively have **cognizance**[5] of all crimes and offenses against this act.

And all marshals and other officers of the United States are required to execute all precepts and orders of the President of the United States issued in pursuance or by virtue of this act.

Section 5: Property Rights of Aliens

And be it further enacted, That it shall be lawful for any alien who may be ordered to be removed from the United States, by virtue of this act, to take with him such part of his goods, **chattels**,[6] or other property, as he may find convenient; and all property left in the United States by any alien, who may be removed, as aforesaid, shall be and remain subject to his order and disposal, in the same manner as if this act had not been passed.

Section 6: Time Limit of the Law

And be it further enacted, That this act shall continue and be in force for and during the term of two years from the passing thereof.

Approved, June 25, 1798.

---

[5] **cognizance**—knowledge.

[6] **chattels**—movable property, such as slaves or farm animals.

Sedition Act

An act for the punishment of certain crimes against the United States.

Section 1: Punishment for Conspiracy Against the Government

Be it enacted by the Senate and House of Representatives of the United States of America in Congress assembled, That if any persons shall unlawfully combine or conspire together, with intent to oppose any measure or measures of the government of the United States, which are or shall be directed by proper authority, or to impede the operation of any law of the United States, or to intimidate or prevent any person holding a place or office in or under the government of the United States, from undertaking, performing or executing his trust or duty; and if any person or persons, with intent as aforesaid, shall counsel, advise or attempt to procure any insurrection, riot, unlawful assembly, or combination, whether such conspiracy, threatening, counsel, advice, or attempt shall have the proposed effect or not, he or they shall be deemed guilty of a high misdemeanor, and on conviction, before any court of the United States having jurisdiction thereof, shall be punished by a fine not exceeding five thousand dollars, and by imprisonment during a term not less than six months nor exceeding five years; and further, at the discretion of the court may be holden to find sureties for his good behavior in such sum, and for such time, as the said court may direct.

Section 2: President's Power to Deport and Imprison Violators

And be it further enacted, That if any person shall write, print, utter, or publish, or shall cause or procure to be written, printed, uttered or published, or shall knowingly and willingly assist or aid in writing, printing, uttering or publishing any false, scandalous and malicious writing or writings against the government of the United States, or either house of the Congress of the United States, or the President of the United States, with intent to defame the said government, or either house of the said Congress, or the said President, or to bring them, or either of them, into contempt or disrepute; or to excite against them, or either or any of them, the hatred of the good people of the United States, or to excite any unlawful combinations therein, for opposing or resisting any law of the United States, or any act of the President of the United States, done in pursuance of any such law, or of the powers in him vested by the Constitution of the United States, or to resist, oppose, or defeat any such law or act, or to aid, encourage or abet any hostile designs of any foreign nation against the United States, their people or government, then such person, being thereof convicted before any court of the United States having jurisdiction thereof, shall be punished by a fine not exceeding two thousand dollars, and by imprisonment not exceeding two years.

Section 3: Rights of the Defendant

And be it further enacted, That if any person shall be prosecuted under this act, for the writing or publishing any **libel**[7] aforesaid, it shall be lawful for the defendant, upon the trial of the cause, to give in evidence in his defense, the truth of the matter contained in the publication charged as a libel. And the jury who shall try the case, shall have a right to determine the law and the fact, under the direction of the court, as in other cases.

---

[7] **libel**—slander; spreading deliberate, false information that harms a person's reputation.

Section 4: Time Limit of the Law

And be it further enacted, That this act shall continue to be in force until March 3, 1801, and no longer. . . .

QUESTIONS TO CONSIDER

1. What rights does the Alien Act give to the president? What is required of ship commanders?

2. Why do you think the punishments are greater for those who violate Section 1 of the Alien Act than for those who break the provisions of Section 2?

3. Why do you think Congress put a time limit on each act?

4. Why, in your opinion, are these acts some of the most controversial in American history?

Early Immigrants

The Pilgrims In 1609, a small group of Puritans left England in search of religious freedom. They spent the next eleven years in Holland before obtaining a grant from the Virginia Company to come to America. They arrived at Cape Cod on November 11, 1620, where they drew up the famous Mayflower Compact and settled at Plymouth on December 21. The winter was mild, but by the following April forty-four Pilgrims had died. Local Native Americans helped those remaining to adapt to life in the New World.

▲
Landing at Plymouth.

◀ Leaving Holland.

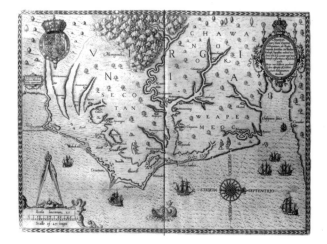

▲

Map of Virginia Coast This 1590 engraving of the Virginia coast was drawn to attract settlers and investors to the Virginia Colony.

From a Map of Virginia In this 1751 illustrated map, slaves are shown packing tobacco into barrels for export to Britain. Tobacco was a major export for the fledgling colonies.

▼

To Be Sold A 1788 print advertises land in Pennsylvania. It was printed in both German and English to appeal to a broad range of immigrants.

▼

The Germans *Among the Protestant groups who moved to America in search of freedom from religious persecution were German immigrants. One such group was invited by the colonial government of Georgia to come and settle a town. Other German immigrants were not so lucky. Many became indentured servants, working for years to pay back the price of their passage to America. Often, they were not allowed to marry, gamble, or sell their possessions during the term of their service.*

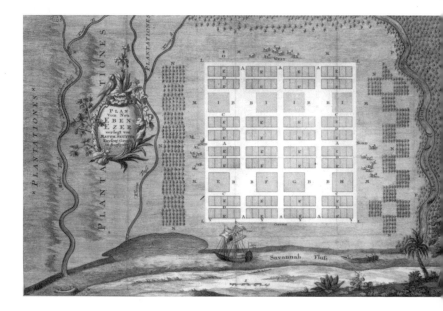

Salzburgische Emigranten

Nichts als das Evangelium
Vertreibt uns ins Exilium.
Verlassen wir das Vaterland,
So sind wir doch in Gottes Hand.

Die Hochfürstliche Haupt und Residenz STADT SALZBURG, von Mitternacht anzusehen.

▲

German Immigrants This 1732 print from the *First History of the Georgia Salzburgers* depicts the homeland and exile of the Salzburgers, who were to settle in Georgia.

◄ **Town Layout** New Ebenezer, Georgia, was settled in 1736 by the persecuted Salzburgers of Bavaria.

▲

Leaving Basel, Germany.

Patterns
and Problems

The Burning of a Convent School

FROM A BOSTON *ATLAS* EDITORIAL

Violence against immigrants is an all-too-familiar pattern of the immigrant experience. With the arrival of Irish Catholics in the 1830s and 1840s, old hostilities between European Protestants and Catholics flared in this country. On August 11, 1834, an angry mob attacked and burned a convent school in Charlestown, Massachusetts. Despite the outrage expressed in the following editorial that appeared in the Boston Atlas, local sentiment sided with the mob. At the trial that followed, only one leader was convicted, and the courtroom audience loudly insulted the prosecution, the nuns, and the Catholic Church. The Massachusetts legislature, under pressure from constituents, dropped its attempts to get financial compensation for the loss of the school building. Catholic churches were forced to add armed security guards, and insurance companies refused to insure some Catholic buildings. The nuns moved to Canada.

From all we can learn, the violence was utterly without cause. The institution[1] was in its very nature unpopular, and a strong feeling existed against it. But there was nothing in the vague rumors that have been idly circulating to authorize or account for the least act of violence. We should state, perhaps, that during the violent scenes that were taking place before the convent—while the mob were breaking the windows and staving[2] in the doors of the institution—and while the fire was blazing upon the hill as a signal to the mob—one or two muskets[3] were discharged from the windows of the nunnery, or some of the buildings in the vicinity.

What a scene must this midnight **conflagration**[4] have exhibited—lighting up the inflamed countenances of an infuriated mob of demons—*attacking a convent of women, a seminary for the instruction of young females*; and turning them out of their beds half naked in the hurry of their flight, and half dead with confusion and terror. And this drama, too, to be enacted on the very soil that afforded one of the earliest places of refuge to the Puritans of New England—themselves flying from religious persecution in the Old World—that their descendants might **wax**[5] strong and mighty, and in their turn be guilty of the same persecution in the New!

We remember no parallel to this outrage in the whole course of history. Turn to the bloodiest incidents of the French Revolution . . . and point us to its equal in unprovoked violence, in brutal outrage, in unthwarted **iniquity**.[6] It is in vain that we search for it. In times of civil **commotion**[7] and general excitement . . . there was

---

[1] institution—school.

[2] staving—bashing.

[3] muskets—guns.

[4] **conflagration**—fire.

[5] **wax**—grow.

[6] **iniquity**—evil.

[7] **commotion**—disturbance (in reference to the French Revolution).

some palliation[8] for violence and outrage—in the tremendously excited state of the public mind. But here there was no such palliation. The courts of justice were open to receive complaints of any improper confinement, or unauthorized coercion. The civil magistrates were, or ought to be, on the alert to detect any illegal restraint, and bring its authors to the punishment they deserve. But nothing of the kind was detected. The whole matter was a cool, deliberate, systematized piece of brutality—unprovoked—under the most provoking circumstances totally unjustifiable and visiting the citizens of the town, and most particularly its magistrates and civil officers, with **indelible**[9] disgrace.

---

[8] palliation—excuse.

[9] **indelible**—permanent; incapable of being removed.

QUESTIONS TO CONSIDER

1. What did the editor find most disturbing about the incident?

2. Why did the editor believe that the burning of the convent school was worse than "the bloodiest incidents" of the French Revolution?

3. What modern examples can you give of unprovoked violence against foreigners or other newcomers to an area?

The First Kennedy in the New World

BY PETER COLLIER AND DAVID HOROWITZ

The struggle for a place in American society is another pattern of immigrant experience. Immigration from Ireland greatly increased during the Great Irish Famine of the 1840s, producing a negative reaction from some Americans who harbored anti-Catholic, anti-Irish feelings. The famous Kennedy family followed a pattern typical of many immigrant groups: The first generation struggled and established the family, building the base for the accomplishments of later generations. Patrick Kennedy came to the United States as a penniless Irishman and only lived for nine years after his arrival. His son, Patrick Joseph Kennedy, became a prominent Boston politician; his grandson, Joseph Kennedy, became a multimillionaire and ambassador to England; and his great-grandson, John Kennedy, became president of the United States. The following excerpt is from The Kennedys: An American Drama.

Exactly how much an Irish tale his story was, how much a metaphor for the rise of the American Irish in general, Joe Kennedy himself would never acknowledge. In the middle of his life, when a Boston newspaper referred to him as an "Irishman" one time too many, he exploded: ". . . I was born in this country! My children were born in this country! What . . . does someone have to do to become an American?" He surrounded himself with tough-talking Boston Irish, yet he had little patience with the easy tears and fusty rhetoric[1] of the stage Irishman who blamed all his woes on discrimination. A self-made, indeed, a self-created man, he was fiercely protective of the individual nature of his accomplishment and had to believe that it was due to temperament, to his own will and philosophy, to what he liked to call "moxie," and not to the sharp and tragic rejection his people had experienced from the time they set foot on American soil. Those who knew him best, however, saw Joe Kennedy as Irish to the core—a logical outcome of the undeclared war that went back at least two hundred years before his birth to the day when a woman named Goody Glover was hanged as a witch on Boston Common because she'd knelt in front of a statue of the Blessed Virgin while telling her beads in the "devil's tongue" of **Gaelic**.[2]

The saga of the Irish in America—a history Joe Kennedy rarely mentioned but never forgot—was part history and part **parable**.[3] The first federal census, in 1790, had listed only 44,000 persons of Irish birth, most of them Ulstermen[4] ("Scotch-Irish," they called themselves) who, as skilled workers and small businessmen, had become outriders for the conquest of the American frontier. Over the next few decades immigration increased, but in 1845 the history of Ireland and America was altered forever when Irish farmers discovered a "blight of unusual character" during the early stages of the potato harvest. The crop had been unreliable for several years but now fresh-

---

[1] fusty rhetoric—old-fashioned speech.

[2] **Gaelic**—the Irish language.

[3] **parable**—simple story illustrating a moral or religious lesson.

[4] Ulstermen—immigrants from northern Ireland, descendants of Protestant Scots, who did not pave the way for the later arrival of the Irish Catholics.

ly dug potatoes turned rotten in hours, decomposing into a gelatinous black ooze with a **putrescent**[5] smell. Livestock fed on the potatoes died; people hungry enough to eat them became violently ill. As the blight spread, the Crown **convened**[6] boards of inquiry whose learned men theorized that the disease was perhaps caused by steam emitted from the locomotives recently introduced into Ireland, by sea-gull droppings the farmers used as fertilizer, or even by **"mortiferous vapors"**[7] rising up from "blind volcanoes" deep in the earth. But if the causes were mysterious (it would later be discovered that the blight had been transmitted by fungus that traveled to Ireland from America), the effects were clear enough. Over the next ten years, the period of the Great Hunger, a million Irish died and another million left their homeland, most of them heading across the sea.

The only parallels of this exodus were the plagues and persecutions of the Old Testament. Packet ships following the example of the Cunard Lines offered fares as low as twelve dollars between Londonderry or Liverpool and New York or Boston; often the tickets were purchased by absentee English landlords anxious to be rid of their starving peasants. The Irish squeezed onto the "coffin ships," floating pest houses of typhus and other diseases, and undertook a voyage as close as any white man ever came to experiencing the dread Middle Passage of the African slave trade. As much as 10 percent of a shipload were likely to die at sea. In 1847, the most disastrous year of all, an estimated 40,000, or 20 percent of those who set out from Ireland, **perished**[8] on the trip. "If crosses and tombs could be erected on water," wrote a U.S. commissioner for emigration, "the whole route of the emigrant vessels from Europe to

---

[5] **putrescent**—rotting.

[6] **convened**—formally assembled.

[7] **"mortiferous vapors"**—deadly fumes.

[8] **perished**—died.

America would long since have assumed the appearance of a crowded cemetery."

Until 1840, Boston had been little more than a debarkation point for immigrants moving on to Canada and the interior of New England. In 1845, in fact, the city's foremost **demographer**[9] confidently asserted that there could be no further increase in the city's population. But over the next ten years, a tidal wave of newcomers—Boston's harbor master claimed to be able to identify another shipload of them as far away as Deer Island just by the smell, piled off their ships, swarmed into Boston, and stayed, a quarter of a million of them. Called "famine Irish" to distinguish them from their predecessors, they were too poor to pay the tolls and fares that would take them out of the waterlocked city; they packed into the reeking Paddyvilles and Mick Alleys, as many as thirty or forty crowding into one tiny cellar, prey to accident and disease that made their death rate as high as it had been in Ireland at the height of the hunger. By 1850 they **comprised**[10] a third of the city's population. Grand with their sudden weight, Boston was about to give birth to the first American immigrant **ghetto**.[11]

Construction companies from all over the country sent to Boston for Irish contract laborers, transporting them to new destinations in railway cars with sealed doors and curtains nailed across the windows. Those who stayed behind became coal heavers and longshoremen, "muckers" and "blacklegs" who dug canals and cleared marshes, remaking the face of the city and giving it an opportunity for unparalleled growth and expansion. (When tourists remarked on the beauty of the cobblestones on Beacon Hill some Irishman was sure to remark, "Those aren't cobblestones, those are Irish hearts.") Yet they remained a people apart, exempt from

---

[9] **demographer**—scientist who keeps population statistics.

[10] **comprised**—made up; were composed of.

[11] **ghetto**—section of a city occupied by a minority group, especially as a result of social, legal, or economic pressure.

New England traditions of transcendental humanism[12] and social uplift which pitied southern Negroes but not their own white slaves. By the 1850s, the infamous NINA—No Irish Need Apply—signs began to appear in Boston, as the antagonists that **culminated**[13] in the Know-Nothing Party and other nativist[14] movements reached a dangerous simmer. Boston's Brahmin[15] elite retreated from the Irish as if from contagion,[16] dividing the city into two cultures, separate and unequal. Mayor Theodore Lyman spoke for those who intended to keep it that way, labeling the Irish "a race that will never be infused with our own, but on the contrary, will always remain distinct and hostile."

This was the atmosphere that twenty-six-year-old Patrick Kennedy found when he arrived in Boston in 1849. He was the third son of a prosperous farmer; the Kennedys of Dugganstown, New Ross, in County Wexford, had eighty acres on which they grew barley and raised beef, and their county was one of the areas least affected by the famine. Unlike the other immigrants, who were literally fleeing death, Patrick had undertaken the journey to improve his fortunes. He left his parents behind, a brother, James, (the oldest son, John, had died [in Ireland] in the battle of Vinegar Hill), and a sister, Mary. He would never see them again; they would never see America.

A handsome, muscular man of medium build, with reddish brown hair and bright blue eyes, Kennedy was not alone when he stepped off the *Washington Irving* at Noddle's Island, a strip of land in Boston Harbor that eventually became East Boston after Irish labor had joined it to the mainland. On board he had met Bridget

---

[12] transcendental humanism—doctrine that takes human experience as the starting point for knowledge of self, God, and the natural world.

[13] **culminated**—ended.

[14] nativist—favoring the established population over recent immigrants.

[15] Brahmin—upper class.

[16] contagion—spreading of disease.

Murphy, also a refugee from County Wexford, and begun his courtship at once. They were married on September 26 of the year they arrived, in the Holy Redeemer Church, by Father John Williams, later to become Boston's archbishop.

The Kennedys went no farther than East Boston, possibly because, like many of their compatriots, they couldn't afford the two pennies it cost to take the ferry across the bay. Patrick sat with other Irishmen on the piers in the shadows of the Cunard liners hoping a short-handed **stevedore**[17] could use him, and, along with other newcomers, walked the crooked streets winding up from the docks looking for work in the **warren**[18] of small shops. After a while he was able to establish himself as a cooper, fashioning yokes and staves for the Conestoga wagons heading west in the great Gold Rush to California and making whiskey barrels destined for the waterfront saloons where the Irish met to exercise their natural sociability and drown their sorrows.

At a time when Americans were beginning to move to cities to escape the smothering traditions of farms and villages, the Irish affirmed the conservative values of their recent rural past in the new urban setting. The tenement apartment, like the Irish farm, was a place where the generations stayed together; the family was the primary unit of emotion and survival. As the New World yielded less to their efforts than they had expected, the Irish turned inward to their kin for support, accenting the "clannishness" the Brahmins found so primitive. Like other immigrants who had left one family behind, Patrick and Bridget Kennedy quickly started another— four children in rapid succession. Mary, Margaret, Johanna, and on January 14, 1858, a son, Patrick Joseph.

---

[17] **stevedore**—person who loads or unloads ships.

[18] **warren**—overcrowded space; named for the area of burrows where rabbits live.

Whatever the fanciful tales told back in the Old Country, there were few rags-to-riches stories for this first generation of Irish. The streets of East Boston were not paved with gold. Instead of a material legacy, they left a sweat equity[19] in America for their children and grandchildren to capitalize on. On November 22, 1858, ten months after the birth of his son, Patrick died of cholera, leaving behind no portraits or documents, just a family. He had survived in Boston for nine years, only five less than the life expectancy for an Irishman in America at mid-century. The first Kennedy to arrive in the New World, he was the last to die in anonymity.

---

[19] sweat equity—investment through working.

QUESTIONS TO CONSIDER

1. Why was the potato famine such an important factor in pushing the Irish to migrate to the United States?

2. In what ways did the conditions surrounding the arrival and early experiences of the Irish in Boston probably promote anti-Irish feelings among established citizens?

3. In what ways was Patrick Kennedy typical of most Irish immigrants of the era? How was he different?

Life in New York Tenement Houses

BY WILLIAM T. ELSING

From the 1830s to the 1850s, the people of northern and western Europe immigrated in large numbers to the Americas. Some settled into crowded sections of New York City and Boston, close to the jobs in the cities. By the 1880s, industrial growth created new demands for labor at the same time that immigrants from southern and eastern Europe began to flee political and economic problems there. As the "old" immigrants prospered and moved out of their tenements, the "new" immigrants moved in. By the early twentieth century, the surge of new immigration from many parts of the globe turned parts of New York City into rows of tenement houses for the latest arrivals. The poor living conditions inspired the establishment of city mission churches to provide services and support for the immigrants. In this excerpt from Gaslight New York Revisited, *William T. Elsing, a city missionary, describes the people and places that were part of this new lifestyle.*

A large number of **tenement-houses**[1] in the lower portion of New York are only a little below the common up-town flat. It is often difficult to tell where the flat leaves off and the tenement begins. You get about as little air and sunshine in the one as in the other. The main difference lies in the number of rooms and the location. If some down-town tenement-houses stood uptown they would be called flats. The word *tenement* is becoming unpopular down-town, and many landlords have dubbed their great caravansaries[2] by the more aristocratic name of "flat," and the term "rooms" has been changed to "apartments."

There are three distinct classes of houses in the tenement-houses; the cheapest and humblest of these is the attic home, which usually consists of one or two rooms, and is found only down-town. These are generally occupied by old persons. Occasionally three or four attic rooms are connected and rented to a family, but as small single rooms are sought after by lonely old people, the landlord often rents them separately. An old lady who has to earn her bread with the needle[3] finds the attic at once the cheapest and best place for her needs. The rent of one or two unfurnished attic rooms ranges from $3 to $5 per month.

A large number of very poor people live in three rooms—a kitchen and two dark bedrooms. Where the family is large the kitchen lounge is opened and converted into a double bed at night. The rent for three rooms is generally from $8 to $12 per month.

The vast majority of respectable working people live in four rooms—a kitchen, two dark bedrooms, and a parlor. These parlors are generally provided with a bed-lounge, and are used as sleeping-rooms at night. The best room is always carpeted and often provided with upholstered

[1] **tenement-houses**—low-rent apartment buildings that barely meet minimum housing standards.

[2] caravansaries—inns for travelers.

[3] earn her bread with the needle—make a living by sewing.

chairs. The walls are generally decorated with family photographs and inexpensive pictures, and in some of them I have found a piano. These parlors compare very favorably with the best room in the house of the average farmer. The rent for four rooms is from $12 to $16 per month.

The rent is an ever-present and unceasing source of anxiety to a great many poor people. The family is sometimes obliged to go half clothed and live on the cheapest and coarsest food in order to provide the rent money. The monthly rent is a veritable sword of Damocles.[4] To a poor woman who dreads the coming of the landlord, the most enticing and attractive description of heaven which I have been able to give is a place where they pay no rent. The landlords are of necessity compelled to be **peremptory**[5] and sometimes arbitrary in their demands. If a landlord were even a little too lenient his tenement property would certainly prove a losing investment. The apparently unreasonable harshness of many landlords is often justifiable, and the only means of securing them against loss. Generally where a good tenant is unable to pay the rent on account of sickness or lack of work the landlord is willing to extend the time a few weeks. I frequently find families who are two or three months **in arrears**.[6] In the majority of cases where dispossess papers[7] are served, the landlord does not know his tenant sufficiently well to trust him, or the tenant is unworthy of trust. Very few of those who are evicted are compelled to take to the street. In most cases sufficient money is collected from friends, neighbors, and charitable people to procure another place of shelter. Occasionally, however, all the worldly possessions of an unfortunate tenant are placed on the street. It is a pathetic sight to see

---

[4] sword of Damocles—threat; according to ancient Greek legend, Damocles was forced to sit under a sword that was suspended by a single hair.

[5] **peremptory**—not allowing argument.

[6] **in arrears**—behind in payments (of rent).

[7] dispossess papers—eviction notices.

a small heap of poor household stuff standing on the sidewalk guarded by the children, while the distressed mother is frantically rushing from one charitable organization to another in search of help.

A poor German woman came to me last year and informed me that her furniture was standing on the sidewalk, and she knew not what would become of her. She had with her a beautiful little girl. The child cried continually, but the mother's distress was too great for tears. She begged me in God's name to help her. I gave her but little encouragement, and dismissed her with a few kind words. She left without heaping abuse on me or cursing the church for its neglect of the poor. A little later I went to the place where she informed me her furniture was and found all her earthly goods on the sidewalk. I inquired of some of her former neighbors about her character, and on being convinced that she was a worthy woman, rented two small rooms in a rear tenement. I found some young street-corner loafers, told them about the woman, and asked them to lend a hand in getting the furniture moved. There is no man so bad that he will not do a good turn for another if you approach him properly. These young roughs went to work with a will, and when the poor woman returned from her last fruitless attempt to collect enough for a new home she found everything arranged. She was thankful and happy. I did not see her until two months later. Then she appeared in as great distress as before, and showed me a new dispossess paper. She informed me that she had failed to find work, everything had been against her, but she hoped to get on her feet if I would once more help her. I told her it was impossible for me to do anything more for her; so she thanked me for my former kindness and departed. That afternoon I heard of a lady in Orange, N.J., who wanted a house-servant and a little girl as waitress. I immediately thought of the German woman and promised if possible to send her out to Orange as soon as arrangements could be made. I was soon in the little rooms of the widow and her daughter and expected to be the bearer of joyful tidings. When I finished she looked sadly at the few scanty pieces of furniture and said:

"If I go to the country what shall I do with the stuff?"

"My good woman," I said, "the stuff is not worth fifty cents; give it to the boys to make a bonfire, and do what I tell you."

"But I have not money enough to leave the city."

I provided the fare, the boys had a glorious time around their fire, and that night, instead of sleeping in her comfortless room, the poor woman was on Orange Mountain. It would have been a losing investment for any landlord to have given an extension of time to that woman, and yet she was a thoroughly worthy person, as the **sequel**[8] proved; her old misery and trouble were at an end. She found a good home and gave perfect satisfaction.

Many other experiences like this, and my constant association with the conditions of tenement-house life, have, of course, led me to certain conclusions as to the best remedies, which I shall reserve for specific mention in the latter part of this article.

The population of the tenement-houses in lower New York is continually changing. There is a constant graduation of the better element. As soon as the circumstances of the people improve they want better homes. A foreigner who took up his **abode**[9] in a tenement-house fifteen or twenty years ago may be perfectly contented with his surroundings, but when his children grow up and earn good wages they are not satisfied with a tenement-house and give the old people no peace until a new home is found. Sometimes a man who has led a bad life reforms and immediately seeks a better home for his wife and children. I know several men who were at one

---

[8] **sequel**—follow-up.

[9] **abode**—home.

time low and degraded drunkards, who would have been satisfied with a pig-sty, who had torn the clothes from their children's backs, the blankets from their beds, and taken them to the pawn-shop to get money for drink; but through the good influences that were thrown around them, the wise counsel of friends, and the saving power of the gospel they became changed men. Their circumstances began to improve, the children were provided with clothes, one piece of furniture after another was brought into the empty rooms, until the place began to look like a home again. These men were charmed with the new life. Home became so dear a place that they were willing to travel an hour each morning and evening in order to make it still more attractive. They began to see the disadvantages of life in a tenement and found a new home on Long Island or in New Jersey.

This constant sifting of the best elements makes religious and **philanthropic**[10] work in lower New York exceedingly difficult and apparently unfruitful, but none the less encouraging and necessary. The fact that the people leave the tenements in search of better homes is the best proof that a good work is being accomplished. A few months ago we celebrated the tenth anniversary of the dedication of one of our city mission churches. There were six hundred present, and out of this number there were only twenty-four who were at the dedication ten years before. While the better class is being constantly sifted out of the tenements, a steady stream of newcomers flows in to take their places.

Successive waves of population follow each other in rapid succession. It is often impossible to tell what the character of the population will be in the next ten years. In 1830 the agents of the New York City Mission visited 34,542 families. Among this number there were only 264 who desired foreign tracts,[11] showing that the population was then

---

[10] **philanthropic**—charitable.

[11] foreign tracts—areas where non-English languages predominate.

almost exclusively American or English-speaking. Now the English language is rarely heard in some of the lower parts of New York, except by the children. That section of the city between the Bowery and East River, Grand and Houston Streets, has been successively occupied by Americans, Irish, Germans, and is now fast coming into the possession of Russian and Polish Jews. The Jewish invasion has been remarkably rapid. Eight years ago I used to see occasionally a Jewish face on the streets or a Jewish sign over the stores. Now the streets swarm with them.

I recently made a careful **canvass**[12] of a typical block and found 300 families composed of 1,424 individuals. The nationalities of the families were as follows: 244 German, 16 Irish, 11 American, 13 Hungarian, 6 Polish, 4 Russian, 2 Bohemian, 1 English, 1 Dutch, and 2 Chinese. Among the 244 German families there were 192 Jews, 38 Protestants, and 14 Roman Catholics. The German Jews are the most highly respected, and on this account many call themselves German who are in reality Russian or Polish Jews. These 300 heads of families are engaged in 72 different trades, occupations, and professions. There are 73 tailors, 17 cigarmakers, 17 storekeepers, 12 peddlers, 11 painters, 9 butchers, and 9 shoemakers in the block. The remaining 65 trades and professions are represented by 148 different persons. Thirty of the heads of families are Roman Catholics, 47 Protestants, and 221 Jews, and 2 have no religion. The Jews do not as a rule mingle to any great extent with the Christians. When they come in large numbers into a street, the Christians gradually withdraw, and the neighborhood finally becomes a Jewish quarter. There are streets in New York where it is a rare thing to find a Christian family.

During the transition period, when a locality is neither Christian nor Jewish, an interesting state of things prevails—a Jewish family, a Roman Catholic family, a pious

---

[12] **canvass**—examination by going house to house.

Protestant family, and a heathen family, as far as religion is concerned, frequently live on the same floor. Suffering appeals to our common humanity. In trouble and sickness these neighbors **render**[13] each other assistance and often become warm friends. I have seen a Jewish woman watching anxiously by the bedside of a dying Christian. A Roman Catholic or Jewish woman will often stand as godmother at the baptism of a Protestant child. A pretty, black-eyed Jewess occasionally captures the heart of a young Roman Catholic or Protestant, and they have come to me to perform the marriage service. Persons of various nations and religious beliefs are sometimes present at a tenement-house funeral. **Bigotry**[14] and national prejudice are gradually broken down and the much-abused tenement becomes a means of promoting the brotherhood of man and the union of Christendom. You may hear daily from the lips of devout Roman Catholics and Jews such words as these: "We belong to a different religion, but we have the same God and hope to go to the same heaven." Such confessions are not often heard in small towns and country districts, but they are frequent in the tenement-houses.

The Jews, who in all ages have been noted for their exclusiveness, are affected by this contact with Christians in the tenement-house. In DeWitt Memorial Church, with which I am connected, an audience of three or four hundred Jews assembles every week to hear Christian instruction. From the standpoint of social science such a gathering every week for the past eighteen months is significant. The Jew in every land has preserved his identity. Persecution has isolated him; when he has been most hated he has flourished, when he has been despised he has prospered. Like the symbolic burning bush, the fires of persecution have not destroyed him. It remains to be seen whether he will preserve his identity in this country,

---

[13] **render**—give; provide.

[14] **Bigotry**—unwillingness to permit the rights or beliefs of others who are different; intolerance.

where, as a citizen, he enjoys equal rights, and where the doors of the public school and the Christian church stand open to Jew and Gentile alike.

Whatever may be the nationality of the parents the children are always thoroughly Americans. The blond-haired, blue-eyed German children; the black-haired, dark-eyed Italians; the little Jews, both dark and blonde, from many lands, are all equally proud of being Americans. A patriotic Irishman gave a beautiful edition of "Picturesque Ireland" to one of the boys in my Sunday-school. The lad looked disappointed. His father asked him why he was not pleased with the present. He answered: "I want a history of the United States." We have a circulating library, patronized almost exclusively by foreigners. The librarian informs me that four boys out of every five call for United States histories.

The most powerful influence at work among the tenement-house population is the public school. Every public school is a great moral lighthouse, and stands for obedience, cleanliness, morality, and patriotism, as well as mental training. When the little children begin to attend the schools their hands and faces are inspected, and if they are not up to the standard, they are sent home for a washing. A boy who is especially dirty is sometimes sent down-stairs with the cleanest boy in school, and told to wash himself until he looks as well as his companion. Such lessons are not soon forgotten, and the result is the public-school children in lower New York present a very respectable appearance. The fresh-air excursions, with many other benefits, promote cleanliness. The heads of the children must be examined before they can enjoy a trip into the country. There is no more beautiful and beneficent[15] charity than this fresh-air work. In two or three weeks the pale-faced children return to the crowded city with renewed health and with larger and better

---

[15] beneficent—producing favorable results.

views of life. I know boys who became so enraptured with green fields, running brooks, waving grain, and life on the farm that they have fully resolved to leave the city when they become men. One little fellow was so anxious to become a farmer that he ran away because his parents would not permit him to leave home.

QUESTIONS TO CONSIDER

1. What are the three distinct classes of homes in the tenement houses? In what ways does each reflect the needs and resources of the renters?

2. What views does the author have of landlords, the "young street roughs," and the dispossessed German woman? What do his views of each have in common?

3. What, according to the author, is the role of the city mission churches in the tenement areas?

4. In what ways does the tenement promote the "brotherhood of man and the union of Christendom"?

▲

"Only an Emigrant" As this drawing from sheet music shows many new immigrants arriving with all their possessions in hand fall victim to unscrupulous men who rush to "help" them.

Russian Immigrants Some immigrants, fleeing war and oppression in their native countries, choose to settle in the American West. These Russian immigrants are bound for Nebraska. ▶

Moving In Italian immigrants carry their belongings on Mulberry Street in the Italian quarter of New York City.

▼

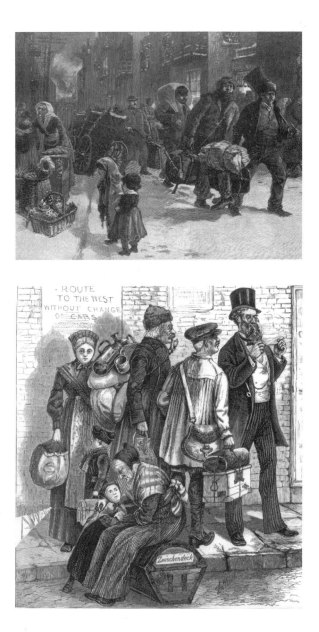

▲

Aboard Ship These women and children were photographed aboard the
S.S. Amsterdam in 1899 on their way to America.

Castle Garden Immigrants came to this New York immigration center to
receive medical inspections, exchange money, purchase tickets for further
transportation, locate missing relatives, and look for jobs. It was replaced by
Ellis Island in 1892. ▶

▲
Welcome to All In this 1880 lithograph from *Puck* magazine, Uncle Sam welcomes immigrants to the United States.

▲

Chinese Immigrants Learning English One of the toughest tasks for immigrants is mastering the English language. Adult education classes provide instruction.

The Biography of a Chinaman

BY LEE CHEW

*Life in urban ghettos is another immigrant pattern. Similar themes
are present in the experiences of most immigrant groups. Between
1850 and 1882, approximately 300,000 Chinese came to the
United States. Many came because of the Taiping Rebellion, an
economically disruptive civil war in China. Others were attracted
by the gold rush in California. They found work as house servants,
miners, and farmers. They helped to build the first transcontinental
railroad, and some went on to become successful businessmen.
However, their willingness to work hard for little pay brought criticism
from many Californians. In 1882, Congress passed the Chinese
Exclusion Act, barring any further immigration from China until
the mid-twentieth century. Lee Chew, who immigrated a few years
before the Exclusion Act was passed, recounts his experiences as
he made his home in turn-of-the-century America. Today, the word
"Chinaman" is characterized by The American Heritage Dictionary
as an "offensive, disparaging term used to describe a Chinese person."*

The village where I was born is situated in the
province of Canton, on one of the banks of the Si-Kiang

River. It is called a village, although it is really as big as a city, for there are about 5,000 men in it over eighteen years of age—women and children and even youths are not counted in our villages.

All in the village belonged to the tribe of Lee. They did not intermarry with one another, but the men went to other villages for their wives and brought them home to their fathers' houses, and men from other villages—Wus and Wings and Sings and Fongs, etc.—chose wives from among our girls.

When I was a baby I was kept in our house all the time with my mother, but when I was a boy of seven I had to sleep at nights with other boys of the village—about thirty of them in one house. The girls are separated the same way—thirty or forty of them sleeping together in one house away from their parents—and the widows have houses where they work and sleep, though they go to their fathers' houses to eat.

My father's house is built of fine blue brick, better than the brick in the houses here in the United States. It is only one story high, roofed with red tiles and surrounded by a stone wall which also encloses the yard. There are four rooms in the house, one large living room which serves for a parlor and three private rooms, one occupied by my grandfather, who is very old and very honorable; another by my father and mother, and the third by my oldest brother and his wife and two little children. There are no windows, but the door is left open all day. All the men of the village have farms, but they don't live on them as the farmers do here; they live in the village, but go out during the day time and work their farms, coming home before dark. My father has a farm of about ten acres, on which he grows a great abundance of things—sweet potatoes, rice, beans, peas, yams, sugar cane, pineapples, bananas, lychee nuts and palms. The palm leaves are useful and can be sold. Men make fans of the lower part of each leaf near the stem, and waterproof coats and hats, and awnings for boats, of the parts that are left when the fans are cut out.

So many different things can be grown on one small farm, because we bring plenty of water in a canal from the mountains thirty miles away, and every farmer takes as much as he wants for his fields by means of drains. He can give each crop the right amount of water.

Our people all working together make these things, the mandarin[1] has nothing to do with it, and we pay no taxes, except a small one on the land. We have our own Government, consisting of the elders of our tribe—the honorable men. When a man gets to be sixty years of age he begins to have honor and to become a leader, and then the older he grows the more he is honored. We had some men who were nearly one hundred years, but very few of them. In spite of the fact that any man may correct them for a fault, Chinese boys have good times and plenty of play. We played games like tag, and other games like shinny and a sort of football called yin.

We had dogs to play with—plenty of dogs and good dogs—that understand Chinese as well as American dogs understand American language. We hunted with them, and we also went fishing and had as good a time as American boys, perhaps better, as we were almost always together in our house, which was a sort of boys' club house, so we had many playmates. Whatever we did we did all together, and our rivals were the boys of other club houses, with whom we sometimes competed in the games. But all our play outdoors was in the daylight, because there were many graveyards about and after dark, so it was said, black ghosts with flaming mouths and eyes and long claws and teeth would come from these and tear to pieces and devour any one whom they might meet.

It was not all play for us boys, however. We had to go to school, where we learned to read and write and to

---

[1] mandarin—government official.

recite the **precepts**[2] of Kong-foo-tsze[3] and the other Sages and stories about the great Emperors of China, who ruled with the wisdom of gods and gave to the whole world the light of high civilization and the culture of our literature, which is the admiration of all nations.

I went to my parents' house for meals, approaching my grandfather with awe, my father and mother with **veneration**[4] and my elder brother with respect. I never spoke unless spoken to, but I listened and heard much concerning the red-haired, green-eyed foreign devils with the hairy faces, who had lately come out of the sea and clustered on our shores. They were wild and fierce and wicked, and paid no regard to the moral precepts of Kong-foo-tsze and the Sages; neither did they worship their ancestors, but pretended to be wiser than their fathers and grandfathers. They loved to beat people and to rob and murder. In the streets of Hong Kong many of them could be seen reeling drunk. Their speech was a savage roar, like the voice of the tiger or the buffalo, and they wanted to take the land away from the Chinese.

Their men and women lived together like animals, without any marriage or faithfulness and even were shameless enough to walk the streets arm in arm in daylight. So the old men said. All this was very shocking and disgusting, as our women seldom were on the street, except in the evenings, when they went with the water jars to the three wells that supplied all the people. Then if they met a man they stood still, with their faces turned to the wall, while he looked the other way when he passed them. A man who spoke to a woman in the street in a Chinese village would be beaten, perhaps killed.

My grandfather told how the English foreign devils had made wicked war on the Emperor, and by means of

---

[2] **precepts**—rules or principles.

[3] Kong-foo-tsze—Confucius, a revered Chinese philosopher who lived from 551 to 479 B.C.

[4] **veneration**—profound respect or reverence.

their enchantments and spells had defeated his armies and forced him to admit their opium, so that the Chinese might smoke and become weakened and the foreign devils might rob them of their land.

My grandfather said that it was well known that the Chinese were always the greatest and wisest among men. They had invented and discovered everything that was good. Therefore the things which the foreign devils had and the Chinese had not must be evil. Some of these things were very wonderful, enabling the red-haired savages to talk with one another, though they might be thousands of miles apart. They had suns[5] that made darkness like day, their ships carried earthquakes and volcanoes to fight for them, and thousands of demons that lived in iron and steel houses spun their cotton and silk, pushed their boats, pulled their cars, printed their newspapers and did other work for them. They were constantly showing disrespect for their ancestors by getting new things to take the place of the old.

I heard about the American foreign devils, that they were false, having made a treaty by which it was agreed that they could freely come to China, and the Chinese as freely go to their country. After this treaty was made China opened its doors to them and then they broke the treaty that they had asked for by shutting the Chinese out of their country.

When I was ten years of age I worked on my father's farm, digging, hoeing, manuring, gathering and carrying the crop. We had no horses, as nobody under the rank of an official is allowed to have a horse in China, and horses do not work on farms there, which is the reason why the roads there are so bad. The people cannot use roads as they are used here, and so they do not make them.

I worked on my father's farm till I was about sixteen years of age, when a man of our tribe came back from

[5] suns—lanterns.

America and took ground as large as four city blocks and made a paradise of it. He put a large stone wall around and led some streams through and built a palace and summer house and about twenty other structures, with beautiful bridges over the streams and walks and roads. Trees and flowers, singing birds, water fowl and curious animals were within the walls.

The man had gone away from our village a poor boy. Now he returned with unlimited wealth, which he had obtained in the country of the American wizards. After many amazing adventures he had become a merchant in a city called Mott Street,[6] so it was said.

When his palace and grounds were completed he gave a dinner to all the people who assembled to be his guests. One hundred pigs roasted whole were served on the tables, with chickens, ducks, geese and such an abundance of dainties that our villagers even now lick their fingers when they think of it. He had the best actors from Hong Kong performing, and every musician for miles around was playing and singing. At night the blaze of the lanterns could be seen for many miles.

Having made his wealth among the barbarians this man had faithfully returned to pour it out among his tribesmen, and he is living in our village now very happy, and a pillar of strength to the poor.

The wealth of this man filled my mind with the idea that I, too, would like to go to the country of the wizards and gain some of their wealth, and after a long time my father consented, and gave me his blessing, and my mother took leave of me with tears, while my grandfather laid his hand upon my head and told me to remember and live up to the **admonitions**[7] of the Sages, to avoid gambling, bad women and men of evil minds, and so to govern my conduct that when I died my ancestors might rejoice to welcome me as a guest on high.

---

[6] Mott Street—heavily Jewish area of Manhattan.

[7] **admonitions**—warnings.

My father gave me $100, and I went to Hong Kong with five other boys from our place and we got steerage passage on a steamer, paying $50 each. Everything was new to me. All my life I had been used to sleeping on a board bed with a wooden pillow, and I found the steamer's bunk very uncomfortable, because it was so soft. The food was different from that which I had been used to, and I did not like it at all. I was afraid of the stews, for the thought of what they might be made of by the wicked wizards of the ship made me ill. Of the great power of these people I saw many signs. The engines that moved the ship were wonderful monsters, strong enough to lift mountains. When I got to San Francisco, which was before the passage of the Exclusion Act,[8] I was half starved, because I was afraid to eat the provisions of the barbarians, but a few days' living in the Chinese quarter made me happy again. A man got me work as a house servant in an American family, and my start was the same as that of almost all the Chinese in this country.

The Chinese laundryman does not learn his trade in China; there are no laundries in China. The women there do the washing in tubs and have no washboards or flat irons. All the Chinese laundrymen here were taught in the first place by American women just as I was taught.

When I went to work for that American family I could not speak a word of English, and I did not know anything about housework. The family consisted of husband, wife and two children. They were very good to me and paid me $3.50 a week, of which I could save $3. I did not know how to do anything, and I did not understand what the lady said to me, but she showed me how to cook, wash, iron, sweep, dust, make beds, wash dishes, clean windows, paint and brass, polish the knives and forks, etc., by doing the things herself and then overseeing my efforts to imitate her. She would take my hands

---

[8] Exclusion Act—the 1882 Chinese Exclusion Act, which barred any further immigration from China.

and show them how to do things. She and her husband and children laughed at me a great deal, but it was all good natured. I was not confined to the house in the way servants are confined here, but when my work was done in the morning I was allowed to go out till lunch time. People in California are more generous than they are here [in New York].

In six months I had learned how to do the work of our house quite well, and I was getting $5 a week and board, and putting away about $4.25 a week. I had also learned some English, and by going to a Sunday school I learned more English and something about Jesus, who was a great Sage, and whose precepts are like those of Kong-foo-tsze.

It was twenty years ago when I came to this country, and I worked for two years as a servant, getting at the last $35 a month. I sent money home to comfort my parents, but though I dressed well and lived well and had pleasure, going quite often to the Chinese theater and to dinner parties in Chinatown, I saved $50 in the first six months, $90 in the second, $120 in the third and $130 in the fourth. So I had $410 at the end of two years, and I was now ready to start in business.

When I first opened a laundry it was in company with a partner, who had been in the business for some years. We went to a town about 500 miles inland, where a railroad was building. We got a board shanty[9] and worked for the men employed by the railroads. Our rent cost us $10 a month and food nearly $5 a week each, for all food was dear and we wanted the best of everything—we lived principally on rice, chickens, ducks and pork, and did our own cooking. The Chinese take naturally to cooking. It cost us about $50 for our furniture and apparatus, and we made close upon $60 a week, which we divided between us. We had to put up with many insults and some frauds, as men would come in and claim parcels that did not belong to them, saying

---

[9] board shanty—small wooden shack.

they had lost their tickets, and would fight if they did not get what they asked for. Sometimes we were taken before Magistrates and fined for losing shirts that we had never seen. On the other hand, we were making money, and even after sending home $3 a week I was able to save about $15. When the railroad construction gang moved on we went with them. The men were rough and prejudiced against us, but not more so than in the big Eastern cities. It is only lately in New York that the Chinese have been able to discontinue putting wire screens in front of their windows, and at the present time the street boys are still breaking the windows of Chinese laundries all over the city, while the police seem to think it a joke.

We were three years with the railroad, and then went to the mines, where we made plenty of money in gold dust, but had a hard time, for many of the miners were wild men who carried revolvers and after drinking would come into our place to shoot and steal shirts, for which we had to pay. One of these men hit his head hard against a flat iron and all the miners came and broke up our laundry, chasing us out of town. They were going to hang us. We lost all our property and $365 in money, which members of the mob must have found.

Luckily most of our money was in the hands of Chinese bankers in San Francisco. I drew $500 and went East to Chicago, where I had a laundry for three years, during which I increased my capital to $2500. After that I was four years in Detroit. I went home to China in 1897, but returned in 1898, and began a laundry business in Buffalo. But the Chinese laundry business now is not as good as it was ten years ago. American cheap labor in the steam laundries has hurt it. So I determined to become a general merchant and with this idea I came to New York and opened a shop in the Chinese quarter, keeping silks, teas, porcelain, clothes, shoes, hats and Chinese provisions, which include shark's fins and nuts, lily bulbs and lily flowers, lychee nuts and other Chinese dainties, but do not include rats, because it would be too expensive to import them. The rat which is eaten by the Chinese is a field animal which lives on rice, grain and sugar cane. Its flesh is delicious. Many Americans who have tasted shark's fin and bird's nest soup and tiger lily flowers and bulbs are firm friends of Chinese cookery. If they could enjoy one of our finer rats they would go to China to live, so as to get some more.

American people eat ground hogs, which are very like these Chinese rats, and they also eat many sorts of food that our people would not touch. Those that have dined with us know that we understand how to live well.

The ordinary laundry shop is generally divided into three rooms. In front is the room where the customers are received, behind that a bedroom and in the back the work shop, which is also the dining room and kitchen. The stove and cooking utensils are the same as those of the Americans.

Work in a laundry begins early on Monday morning—about seven o'clock. There are generally two men, one of whom washes while the other does the ironing. The man who irons does not start in till Tuesday, as the clothes are not ready for him to begin till that time. So he has Sundays and Mondays as holidays. The man who does the washing finishes up on Friday night, and so he has Saturday and Sunday. Each works only five days a week, but those are long days—from seven o'clock in the morning till midnight.

During his holidays the Chinaman gets a good deal of fun out of life. There's a good deal of gambling and some opium smoking, but not so much as Americans imagine. Only a few of New York's Chinamen smoke opium. The habit is very general among rich men and officials in China, but not so much among poor men. I don't think it does as much harm as the liquor that the Americans drink. There's nothing so bad as a drunken man. Opium doesn't make people crazy.

Gambling is mostly *fan tan*,[10] but there is a good deal of poker, which the Chinese have learned from Americans and can play very well. They also gamble with dominoes and dice. The fights among the Chinese and the operations of the hatchet men[11] are all due to gambling. Newspapers often say that there are feuds between the six companies, but that is a mistake. The six companies are purely benevolent societies, which look after the Chinaman when he first lands here. They represent the six southern provinces of China, where most of our people are from, and they are like the German, Swedish, English, Irish and Italian societies which assist emigrants. When the Chinese keep clear of gambling and opium they are not blackmailed, and they have no trouble with hatchet men or any others.

About 500 of New York's Chinese are Christians, the others are Buddhists, Taoists, etc., all mixed up. These haven't any Sunday of their own, but keep New Year's Day and the first and fifteenth days of each month, when they go to the temple in Mott Street.

In all New York there are only thirty-four Chinese women, and it is impossible to get a Chinese woman out here unless one goes to China and marries her there, and then he must collect affidavits to prove that she really is his wife. That is in [the] case of a merchant. A laundryman can't bring his wife here under any circumstances, and even the women of the Chinese Ambassador's family had trouble getting in lately.

Is it any wonder, therefore, or any proof of the demoralization of our people if some of the white women in Chinatown are not of good character? What other set of men so isolated and so surrounded by alien and prejudiced people are more moral? Men, wherever they may be, need the society of women, and among the white women of Chinatown are many excellent and faithful wives and mothers.

---

[10] *fan tan*—Chinese game of chance.

[11] hatchet men—men hired to commit murder. Chew is referring to the activities of gangsters who ran the gambling operations.

Recently there has been organized among us the Oriental Club, composed of our most intelligent and influential men. We hope for a great improvement in social conditions by its means, as it will discuss matters that concern us, bring us in closer touch with Americans and speak for us in something like an official manner.

Some fault is found with us for sticking to our old customs here, especially in the matter of clothes, but the reason is that we find American clothes much inferior, so far as comfort and warmth go. The Chinaman's coat for the winter is very durable, very light and very warm. It is easy and not in the way. If he wants to work he slips out of it in a moment and can put it on again as quickly. Our shoes and hats also are better, we think, for our purposes, than the American clothes. Most of us have tried the American clothes, and they make us feel as if we were in the stocks.[12]

I have found out, during my residence in this country, that much of the Chinese prejudice against Americans is unfounded, and I no longer put faith in the wild tales that were told about them in our village, though some of the Chinese, who have been here twenty years and who are learned men, still believe that there is no marriage in this country, that the land is infested with demons and that all the people are given over to general wickedness. I know better. Americans are not all bad, nor are they wicked wizards. Still, they have their faults, and their treatment of us is outrageous.

The reason why so many Chinese go into the laundry business in this country is because it requires little capital and is one of the few opportunities that are open. Men of other nationalities who are jealous of the Chinese, because he is a more faithful worker than one of their people, have raised such a great outcry about Chinese cheap labor that they have shut him out of working on farms or in factories or building railroads or making streets or digging sewers. He cannot practice any trade,

---

[12] in the stocks—confined.

and his opportunities to do business are limited to his own countrymen. So he opens a laundry when he quits domestic service.

The treatment of the Chinese in this country is all wrong and mean. It is persisted in merely because China is not a fighting nation. The Americans would not dare to treat Germans, English, Italians or even Japanese as they treat the Chinese, because if they did there would be a war.

There is no reason for the prejudice against the Chinese. The cheap labor cry was always a falsehood. Their labor was never cheap, and is not cheap now. It has always commanded the highest market price. But the trouble is that the Chinese are such excellent and faithful workers that bosses will have no others when they can get them. If you look at men working on the street you will find an overseer for every four or five of them. That watching is not necessary for Chinese. They work as well when left to themselves as they do when someone is looking at them.

It was the jealousy of laboring men of other nationalities—especially the Irish—that raised all the outcry against the Chinese. No one would hire an Irishman, German, Englishman or Italian when he could get a Chinese, because our countrymen are so much more honest, industrious, steady, sober and **painstaking**.[13] Chinese were persecuted, not for their vices, but for their virtues. There never was any honesty in the pretended fear of leprosy or in the cheap labor scare, and the persecution continues still, because Americans make a mere practice of loving justice. They are all for money making, and they want to be on the strongest side always. They treat you as a friend while you are prosperous, but if you have a misfortune they don't know you. There is nothing substantial in their friendship.

---

[13] **painstaking**—careful and diligent.

Wu-Ting-Fang[14] talked very plainly to Americans about their ill treatment of our countrymen, but we don't see any good results. We hoped for good from Roosevelt[15]—we thought him a brave and good man, but yet he has continued the exclusion of our countrymen, though all other nations are allowed to pour in here—Irish, Italians, Jews, Poles, Greeks, Hungarians, etc. It would not have been so if Mr. McKinley[16] had lived.

Irish fill the almshouses and prisons and orphan asylums, Italians are among the most dangerous of men, Jews are unclean and ignorant. Yet they are all let in, while Chinese, who are sober, or duly law abiding, clean, educated and industrious, are shut out. There are few Chinamen in jails and none in the poor houses. There are no Chinese tramps or drunkards. Many Chinese here have become sincere Christians, in spite of the persecution which they have to endure from their heathen countrymen. More than half the Chinese in this country would become citizens if allowed to do so, and would be patriotic Americans. But how can they make this country their home as matters now are! They are not allowed to bring wives here from China, and if they marry American women there is a great outcry.

All Congressmen acknowledge the injustice of the treatment of my people, yet they continue it. They have no backbone.

Under the circumstances, how can I call this my home, and how can anyone blame me if I take my money and go back to my village in China?

---

[14] Wu-Ting-Fang—a Chinese diplomat.

[15] Roosevelt—Theodore Roosevelt, President from 1901 to 1909.

[16] Mr. McKinley—William McKinley, President from 1897 to 1901, whose assassination made Theodore Roosevelt the President.

QUESTIONS TO CONSIDER

1. What was the author's life in his village in China like? In what important ways was it different from his life in the United States?

2. Why did the Chinese consider themselves to be superior to the English and Americans?

3. What inspired the author to immigrate to America?

4. What skills and resources did Lee Chew need to open his business? How did he build his success?

5. Why, according to the author, were turn-of-the-century Americans prejudiced against the Chinese?

The Spirit of the Girl Strikers

BY MIRIAM FINN SCOTT

*Labor unions for skilled workers were organized during the late
1800s, but by the early twentieth century, the vast majority of new
immigrants worked in crowded factories with owners who strongly
resisted unionization. Among the most unfortunate of these workers
were young girls who labored in the garment industry in New York
City. They were inspired to organize a strike after the famous
Triangle Shirtwaist Factory fire in 1913, in which hundreds of young
immigrant women lost their lives. The shocking working conditions
in the factory moved many New Yorkers to support the girls' cause,
helping to make their strike a success.*

The "Grand American Palace" was packed with a
strangely unaccustomed crowd. Every night "Professor"
Somebody's orchestra (the "professor" and two pasty-
faced helpers) dispensed music from the little platform
in the corner, and some scores of work-worn immigrant
boys and girls, at so much per head, struggled and
giggled through the waltz and the two-step. But now,

instead of these weary revelers, from gaudy wall to gaudy wall were jammed girls with determined, workaday faces. Strikers they were—a group of shirt-waist makers,[1] whose strike in New York has been the biggest and most bitter strike of women in the history of American labor troubles.

And the faces of this group were fixed on the "Professor's" stage, and on that stage stood a slight, pale girl of perhaps nineteen, her dark eyes flashing. "Girls, from the bottom of my heart," she cried, "I beg you not to go back to work. We are all poor, many of us are suffering hunger, none of us can afford to lose a day's wages. But only by fighting for our rights, and fighting all together, can we better our miseries; and so let us fight for them to the end!"

The strikers applauded long, and on scores of other East Side dance-halls at the time when the strike was at its height and forty thousand girls were out, just so at this same hour were other speakers applauded by other groups; and by meetings such as this was the spirit kept in the girls for their remarkable fight. When the girl left the platform, I edged my way to her and asked her for her story. She had come from Russia, she told me—come with her parents, who had found life in the land of the Czar no longer endurable.

"Close your eyes and point to any girl in this hall," said the little shirt-waist maker, "and my story will be her story. We are all the same. Why do we strike? I will tell you where we work, how we work; from that per-haps you will understand. My shop is a long and narrow loft on the fifth floor of the building, with the ceiling almost on our heads. In it one hundred electric-power machines are so closely packed together that, unless I am always on the lookout, my clothes or hair or hand is likely to catch in one of the whizzing machines. In the shop it

---

[1] shirt-waist makers—dressmakers.

is always night. The windows are only on the narrow ends of the room, so even the few girls who sit near them sew by gaslight most of the time, for the panes are so dirty the weak daylight hardly goes through them. The shop is swept only once a week; the air is so close that sometimes you can hardly breathe. In this place I work from eight to six o'clock six days in the week in the ordinary season; and in the busy season, when we are compelled to work nights and Sundays, I put in what equals eight work-days in the week. Thirty minutes is allowed for lunch, which I must eat in the dressing-room four flights above the shop, on the ninth floor. These stairs I must always climb; the elevator, the boss says, is not for the shop-girls.

"I began as a shirt-waist maker in this shop five years ago. For the first three weeks I got nothing, though I had already worked on a machine in Russia. Then the boss paid me three dollars a week. Now, after five years' experience, and I am considered a good worker, I am paid nine. But I never get the nine dollars. There are always 'charges' against me. If I laugh, or cry, or speak to a girl during work hours, I am fined ten cents for each 'crime.' Five cents is taken from my pay every week to pay for benzine which is used to clean waists that have been soiled in the making; and even if I have not soiled a waist in a year, I must pay the five cents just the same. If I lose a little piece of lining, that possibly is worth two cents, I am charged ten cents for the goods and five cents for losing it. If I am one minute late, I am fined one cent, though I get only fifteen cents an hour; and if I am five minutes late, I lose half a day's pay. Each of these things seems small, I know, but when you only earn ninety dimes a week, and are fined for this and fined for that, why, a lot of them are missing when pay day comes, and you know what it means when your money is the only regular money that comes in a family of eight."

She told me other grievances, many of them. And as I went from meeting to meeting talking to the girls, as

I walked with them on picket duty, I found that she had spoken truly when she said, "My story is their story."

An olive-skinned Italian beauty of eighteen said to me: "If only I speak the English good, I go and tell everybody what awful place is our shop. Just like a prison, the doors always locked. When we are very, very sick sometime, we never can go home; always the bosses scream, say bad words to us. When we no got work we must sit, sit in the shop all day, and wait, and sometime we have just thirty-five cents at the end of the week. Oh, so bad! so bad!"

The "fining" system just referred to is not the only method by which, the girls claim, their meager wages are subtracted from. "There ain't nothing too low for my boss to do to make a few extra cents' profit," said another girl. "He ain't ashamed to do plain stealing from us girls. In our shop we have no books to mark down our work— just little slips of paper, checks, are given us when we turn in a bundle of work. For these slips we are given money at the end of the week. The boss has these slips made small purposely, so they'll be easier to lose. One week I lost two of these tiny pieces of paper, and I could not get one cent for the work I had done. It was half my week's wages. Every day some of us lose these tickets. But our loss is the boss's gain, so he won't change the system."

There is one very simple explanation for the wretched conditions under which the girls have worked—they have been very easy to exploit. Ninety per cent of the workers are Russian and Italian girls between eighteen and twenty-five. These girls enter the shop almost immediately after landing in America. They come from great poverty and oppression, where they were compelled to accept conditions without complaint. And so, accustomed to fear and [being forced to] obey, these girls have for years suffered their grievances here, and kept silent.

Now and then in the past there have been attempts made by the workers to fight the conditions, but the individual uprisings had no effect. The spirit of discontent among the workers grew, and continued to grow deeper and wider; it set the girls thinking, and finally they realized that the only possible remedy for these conditions was for all of them to stand together and make common demands—to organize a strong union and gain recognition for it.

Everywhere was **ferment**.[2] The girls were ripe for the strike, as was shown by the quickness and unanimity with which the girls responded to the call for the strike. But, even so, among the girls were leaders each of whom roused and led her own group of less militant comrades. Among these were Eva Goldstein, and this is her story of how she "called down" her shop:

"I knew our girls were dissatisfied. I knew other shops were already on strike. I knew it only needed some one to talk to the girls a little and they would join the strikers. So I began to talk to the girls whenever I got the chance. I went to their houses in the evening; I met them early in the morning. At first some girls would not listen to me; they were afraid to lose their 'grand job.' But at last we all agreed. Tuesday morning we came to work as usual, but after we were thirty minutes at our machines I got up and called to them:

"Girls, other waist-makers are on strike! Will you join them?"

"Every girl got up from her machine. As we were all starting for the door the boss rushed in and began to shout. 'Sit down; sit down, girls.' But not one of us took our seat. The boss came over to me; he was very mad. 'I know you are the trouble-maker,' he said. 'Tell the girls to sit down; tell me what you want. Here is an agreement,' and he drew out a sheet of paper and a pencil from his pocket. 'I will sign this agreement. I'll give you a raise. If you sign that, too, you and the girls won't have to strike in this shop.'

[2] **ferment**—turmoil.

"I just smiled at him, for I knew it wasn't a real agreement, but just a trick, a fake, and I said, 'Mr. —, if you are willing to settle, you must go to the union headquarters to sign the agreement. I have no right to sign.' Then I just said, 'Girls, are you coming?' and we all walked out and left him there alone."

Scores of shops have gone out with no demands except the recognition of the union, for in some shops the conditions are far superior to the average. Hundreds and hundreds of girls who are striking left their work in pure sympathy, with no personal grievances whatever. "Just because I am better treated than the other girls, that's more reason why I should be on strike," argued Annie Silver. "This is not just a strike for self. Only by all standing together can we get better conditions for all."

Annie is the swiftest sample-trimmer of the Blank Waist Company. She works at a fixed salary of $5 a week. In three years Annie missed only one day's work, and there were three good reasons for such faithfulness to her job—a blind mother and two little sisters. After the first week on strike, Annie went back to the shop to get wages still due her. The boss, knowing her circumstances, tempted her to return to work by offering her a raise of $5 a week, but to that Annie promptly replied: "Mr. Baum, you cannot buy my conscience for money!"

It is ten long, bitter weeks since Annie went out; she has been picketing, speaking, organizing every day since. During all these weeks she never had more than two meals a day, often only one; lately days pass practically without her tasting food. But the blind mother and two little ones still have their food and roof, and do not know of Annie's sacrifices.

But to appreciate what sufferings these girls are undergoing for the sake of better conditions in the future, one must know a little of how they live in times when there is no strike. Some of the girls earn but $3 or $4 a week; a few exceptionally clever girls, working in exceptionally well run shops, earn as high as $20 and $25. The story circulated by the bosses that some of the girls get $35 and $40 a week is false, and the evidence by which they seek to substantiate the story amounts to a mere trick of bookkeeping. The average wages for the forty thousand workers is $9, and this is not for fifty-two weeks in the year, but only for the busy season, a period of about three months. During six months of the year, the average is from $3 to $5 a week, and during the remaining three months the girls are practically idle. So the average wage is in reality only about $5 a week, and on this amount the girls must feed, clothe, and house themselves. How do they manage to exist in New York, where the cost of living is so high?

This is how. Most of the strikers board with a "missus" who lives in a miserable four-room flat in an East Side tenement. Besides the missus, her husband, and numerous children, the flat is shared by two or three boarders. The charge is $3 a week. This entitles the boarder to a cot in the sitting-room, a breakfast of coffee and bread without butter, and a supper of cheap meat, bread, and tea. The boarder must provide her own lunch, usually at a cost of from three to six cents. She does her own laundry of nights, makes some of her clothes on Sundays, and does without necessaries most of the time. Such is her life in the fat times of peace.

The period of any strike is always a time of suffering and sacrifice for the workers—for at his greatest prosperity, the worker's hand barely reaches his mouth; but this strike of girls has been distinguished by the added suffering, yes and disgrace, inflicted by the brutality of the police, by the brutality of thugs hired by bosses and protected by the police, and by the shameless brutality of the police court magistrates. So flagrant has been the harshness of the magistrates that great numbers of prominent New York men and women, people who usually take no interest in labor struggles, have risen in protest—and this very harshness and brutality, whose seeming purpose was to browbeat the girls into submission, has served to gain for them a wider sympathy, and is materially aiding them in winning their long fight.

Almost every shirt-waist maker who has taken an active part in the strike—and few indeed there are who have not—has some terrible experience to tell of her contact with the representatives of the law. Fannie Goldmark has deep-set, sorrowful eyes, yet she was calm and often smiled as she told me her story. She was born at Kishineff, and lost every member of her immediate family in the great massacre.[3] She had heard of America as the land of liberty and justice, and in fear and hope she fled from Kishineff. Arrived in New York, she at once entered a shop and learned shirt-waist making. In Russia she had been a student, and had gone about among the Russian workmen trying to spread the lesson of organization. So, when the strike broke out, she was among the first to enlist. She was very successful as a speaker, as an organizer, and particularly as a picket. While picketing she was arrested three times. The first two charges against her were for "disturbing the peace," when in fact she was quietly, and legally, walking up and down in front of her shop. Each of these two times she was fined five dollars. The third time she was arrested she was dragged to the station-house like a disorderly woman, on the charge of assaulting a six-foot policeman. As a matter of fact, the policeman tripped her, and she fell off the sidewalk near the place where the policeman stood. She was thrown into a cell and for ten hours she was absolutely refused permission to communicate with the union about her arrest unless she paid fifty cents for the telephone message, which amount she did not possess. At the trial she was severely reprimanded by

---

[3] The Kishineff massacre was a violent raid in 1903 of Jewish areas by Russian soldiers; it was part of the czar's forceful removal of Jews from Russia.

the magistrate and warned that the next time "her foot entered the court-room, she would land in the workhouse."

It was nearly midnight when Fannie, dizzy with weariness, hunger, and cold, reached the flat of her "missus." But her key no longer fitted the door. In the very dim light she saw her few belongings stacked up in the hallway. She had been dispossessed and had a home no more.

She went back into the night. Finally she found a sleeping-place with a friend who lives with her parents. And now, despite it all, she is still picketing, morning, noon, and night.

QUESTIONS TO CONSIDER

1. What answer did the "little shirt-waist maker" give to her question, "Why do we strike?"

2. Why was it particularly easy for the factory owners to exploit the girls?

3. Why did the strikes require so much courage on the part of the workers?

Zoot Suit War

FROM *TIME* MAGAZINE

Violence as a pattern in immigrant life sometimes erupted out of the bitterness and anger of an oppressed group. By the 1940s, many Latinos lived in poverty-stricken sections of Los Angeles and other major California cities. From these "barrios"—Latino ghettos—came youthful street gangs, the most famous of which was known as the "Pachucos." In 1942, the Pachucos made headline news when a member was killed in a fight over a girlfriend. As a result of the publicity, twenty-four Mexican boys were arrested and nine convicted of second-degree murder. They were later released, but this incident, known as the "Sleepy Lagoon" case, was bitterly remembered in the barrio for many years. A year later, racial tensions erupted into the "Zoot Suit" riots, named after the Pachucos' unusual outfits. The riot took place amid World War II tensions. It began as a fist fight between a gang of Latino boys and American sailors in downtown Los Angeles and continued for days, leaving hundreds injured and a residue of racial hatred.

For two nights the mobs of soldiers and sailors had found poor hunting. In their caravans of cabs and private cars they had toured the Mexican sections, armed with sticks and weighted ropes, crashing into movie houses, looking for zoot-suited *pachucos*, the little Mexican-American youths. But they had found only a few dozen, and not all of them even wore zoot suits. They had broken the jaw of a 13-year-old boy. Said the boy, in the hospital:

"So our guys wear tight bottoms on their pants and those bums wear wide bottoms. Who . . . they fighting, Japs[1] or us?"

One *Panser*[2] division of the cab-and-car attack had rolled down a Mexican district side street, past the rows of mean, ramshackle frame houses. But they had only found a few victims to beat. One of them was a 17-year-old Russian boy, Pete Nogikios, talking on a street corner to two Mexicans. The Mexicans fled. Pete stood still. The sailors beat him to the ground.

Scores of Mexican youths had been stripped of their pants (some of them on the stages of movie houses), beaten and then arrested by the Los Angeles police for "vagrancy" and "rioting." (The police practice was to accompany the caravans in police cars, watch the beatings and then jail the victims. Their orders apparently were to let the Shore Patrol and the Military Police handle the rioting sailors. The service police were futile.)

But now the rioting seemed to be diminishing. The zoot-suiters lay low, the sailors and soldiers had seemingly wreaked sufficient revenge for the several occasions when zoot-hoodlums had attacked and robbed them.

Hearst Moves In.

But then the press took up the story. The Hearst newspapers, the Los Angeles *Examiner* and the *Herald & Express*, and Harry Chandler's Los Angeles *Times* began to blaze. Late-afternoon editions printed black-faced

---

[1] Japs—derogatory term used to describe the Japanese people during the war.

[2] *Panser*—armored; a reference to the German tanks of World War II.

leads[3] about a **purported**[4] anonymous call to head-quarters: "We're meeting 500 strong tonight and we're going to kill every cop we see." The Hearst *Herald & Express* bannered: ZOOTERS THREATEN L.A. POLICE.

The Mob Moves In.

That night all Los Angeles stayed downtown to see the fun. The darkness came to the fog-chilled streets, the sidewalks and streets were jammed with expectant servicemen and civilians. Shore Patrol cars, Military Police and police and sheriff's cars patrolled in force.

Scores of cars loaded with soldiers and sailors poured into the area. Soon after dark a mob formed, surged down Broadway, crashed into the Orpheum Theater, went down the aisles shouting for pachucos to stand up. In the balcony the mob found 17-year-old Enrico Herrera, sitting with his girl. He and others were dragged downstairs to the street; the citizenry pushed back to give them room while he was beaten and stripped naked. The crowd howled. When the sailors had finished, the police dutifully edged up, took Herrera to the hospital.

The mob went happily down Broadway, repeating in every theater, the Rialto, the Tower, Loew's. Others topped streetcars, pulled off zooters, Mexicans or just dark-complexioned males. On went the mob, ripping pants, beating the young civilians, into the Arcade, the Roxy, the Cameo, the Broadway, the Central and the New Million Dollar theaters. The mood of officialdom (the Shore Patrol, the Military Police, the city police, the sheriff's office) seemed **complaisant**.[5]

---

[3] black-faced leads—opening paragraphs of news stories printed in bold type.

[4] **purported**—assumed to be; supposed.

[5] **complaisant**—good-natured.

Hoodlumism

The mob split all over Los Angeles, to Watts, Belvedere, Boyle Heights, El Monte, Baldwin Park, Montebello, San Gabriel—anywhere that Mexicans lived.

Hearst's *Examiner* kept pounding: *"Police Must Clean Up L.A. Hoodlumism."* The first paragraph of an editorial said:

"Riotous disturbances of the past week in Los Angeles by zoot-suit hoodlums have inflicted a deep and humiliating wound on the reputation of this city."

California's zoot-suit war was a shameful example of what happens to wartime emotions without wartime discipline.

Some of Los Angeles' young Mexicans organized into zoot-suit "gangs" that were the equivalent of boys' gangs almost anywhere, had got out of hand: they had robbed and used their knives on some lone sailors on dark side streets. But probably the trouble could have been ended right there. One who thought so was Eduardo Quevedo, a plump, cigar-chewing, shock-headed amateur sociologist, president of the Coordinating Council for Latin Americans, member of the Citizens' Committee on Latin American youth.

Eight months ago, Goodman Quevedo went to work to stop youthful hoodlumism, started a kind of grown-up Boys Club for the zooters. He knew that they represented a basic American problem: the second generation.[6] Their fathers and mothers were still Mexicans at heart. They themselves were Americans—resented and looked down on by other Americans. Jobless, misunderstood in their own homes and unwelcome outside them, they had fallen into the companionship of misery. They dressed alike, in the most exaggerated and outlandish costume they could afford: knee-length

---

[6] second generation—children of immigrants born in the United States. The first generation are the foreign born immigrants.

coats, peg-top trousers, yard-long watch chains, "duck-tail" haircuts.

If the pachucos had asked for trouble, they got more than was coming to them last week. The military authorities were notably lax (all shore and camp leave could easily have been cancelled), the Los Angeles police apparently looked the other way. The press, with the exception of the *Daily News* and Hollywood *Citizen-News*, helped whip up the mob spirit. And Los Angeles, apparently unaware that it was **spawning**[7] the ugliest brand of mob action since the coolie race riots of the 1870s,[8] gave its **tacit**[9] approval.

---

[7] **spawning**—starting.

[8] coolie race riots of the 1870s—riots caused by conflict over Chinese immigration.

[9] **tacit**—unspoken; silent; implied.

QUESTIONS TO CONSIDER

1. What did soldiers and sailors find so objectionable about the "zoot-suiters"? What did "youthful hoodlumism" have to do with their attitude?

2. How does the article criticize the police?

3. How, in your opinion, could the riot have been prevented?

4. What is the meaning of this comment in the article: "California's zoot-suit war was a shameful example of what happens to wartime emotions without wartime discipline"?

Life as an Alien

BY MERI NANA-AMA DANQUAH

The immigrant experience frequently brings with it a "half and half" feeling of not fully belonging to either the culture of the new country or the old. With one foot in each culture, immigrants are distanced from people that they grew up with. The process of adjusting completely to their new lives is often slow and difficult. In the following selection written in the 1970s, Meri Nana-Ama Danquah, an African immigrant from Ghana who was living in Los Angeles, explores her life as an "alien" and contemplates the emotional effects of living in the United States for many years without becoming a citizen.

I don't know where I come from. When people ask me, I have to stop and wonder what it is they really want to know about me. Do they want to know where I was born, where I grew up, where I have lived as an adult, where I live now? It troubles me to be so scattered, so fragmented, so far removed from a center. I am all and I am nothing. At the same time. Once, a long time ago, when I believed that answers were as easy as smiles, someone told me that home is where the heart is.

Perhaps this is true. Love has always been a magnet. It is half the sky, the raggedy part that needs to be held up and saved. It is a name as long as history with enough vowels for each of its children to claim. It is the memory of wearing open-toed shoes in December. Of mango juice running a straight river from your hand to your elbow.

Love is a plate of steamed white rice and pig's-feet stew. As a child, this was my favorite meal. I would sit at the dining table, my legs swinging back and forth, and hum as I scooped the food into my mouth with my hand. I always ate the rice first, saving the meat in a towering heap on the side for last. After I had finished the rice, I would wash it down with some water or Coco-Rico, this coconut-milk soda my mum used to buy. Then I would greedily dig into the pile of pork and choose the largest piece. When my teeth had grazed all the flesh clean off the bone, I would hold it to my lips and suck it dry of its juice. I would bite down hard until it broke in half and I could touch the marrow with the tip of my tongue. Right then, right there, I knew my world was complete.

Several years ago, in what I can only assume was a temporary loss of sanity, I decided to become a vegetarian. Swept into the New Age organic, fat-free health obsessions of Los Angeles, the city in which I live, I vowed to never again eat another piece of meat. Not fish, not chicken, and certainly never pork. In preparation for what I believed would be a permanent change of lifestyle, I spent the morning of my first meatless day in the produce section of the supermarket stocking up on lettuce and carrots, and at the bookstore buying books like *Diet for a New America*. Throughout the day, whenever I grew hungry, I would pull out a carrot stick or rice cake and nibble, often squeezing my lips into a tight purse of dissatisfaction after swallowing. What I really wanted to be eating was fried chicken. It felt strange to not eat meat anymore; nothing I took in seemed to fill me.

"You'll get used to the change," a friend promised. "Pretty soon, the idea of putting that stuff in your body'll turn your stomach." We were at an Indian restaurant celebrating my newfound diet. I pondered what she said, scanned the menu, reading only the selections listed under the heading "Vegetarian," and ordered the Saag Paneer with Basmati Rice. When my dinner arrived, a gentle **nostalgia**[1] descended upon me. The food—a creamy stew of chopped spinach—resembled kontumare, a Ghanaian dish I very much enjoy. I was, all at once, swept up by the force of habit—the habit, that is, of moving my head, torso, and legs in rhythm to a series of closed-mouth "Yums." Except the pot of gold at the end of my culinary rainbow was missing. There was no meat. And that absence left me feeling so cheated out of an **integral**[2] part of the experience I was having that before returning to my apartment I stopped by an uncle's house and begged the leftover remains of his curried goat dinner.

My attempt to be an **herbivore**[3] was but one in a long list of numerous attempts I have made to create or "try out" a new identity. In my twenty-four years of living in America, I have adapted to all sorts of changes. I have housed many identities inside the one person I presently call myself, a person I know well enough to admit that I don't know at all. Like a **chameleon**,[4] I am ever-changing, able to blend without detection into the colors and textures of my surroundings, a skill developed out of a need to belong, a longing to be claimed. Once, home was a place, perhaps the only place, where I imagined that I really did belong, where I thought myself whole. That is not so anymore, at least not in the

---

[1] **nostalgia**—sentimental longing for what is past or far away; homesickness.

[2] **integral**—essential.

[3] **herbivore**—vegetarian.

[4] **chameleon**—lizard whose skin color changes to match the surface it is on, to protect it from its enemies.

home that I grew up believing was mine. That word, "home," and all it represents, have shifted in meaning too many times.

From the age of six, when I left Ghana and arrived in Washington, D.C., to be with my mother, who had been in the States already for three years, it was quite clear that someday we would return. There was always talk of going back. There were always plans being made, sentences being spoken that began with words like "When I go home. . . . " Even after my father joined us, America was still just a place of temporary existence, not home. And in consideration of our imminent departure, **assimilation**[5] was frowned upon. My parents tried to fan the flames of our culture within me, in hopes that it would grow into a raging fire and burn fully any desire I had to become an American.

English was spoken only in the presence of people who could not communicate in any of our languages (Ga or Twi). It wasn't as if my parents forbade me to speak English, but if I addressed either of them in English, the response I got was always in Ga. These days my father, now remarried to an American, speaks to me primarily in English, unless I speak to him first in Ga, and even then chances are he will respond in English. My mother still insists upon conversing with me in Ga. When it appeared as though I was losing fluency, she became **adamant**[6] and uncompromising about this; in her mind, to forget one's mother tongue was to place the final **sever**[7] in the umbilical cord. I do believe that she was right, but over the years I have praised and cursed her for this.

Although we didn't speak English in my house, we surely did sing in it. Music was a constant. We listened

---

[5] **assimilation**—the process of becoming part of mainstream American culture.

[6] **adamant**—firm; totally unyielding.

[7] **sever**—cut. The umbilical cord that connects a baby to its mother in the womb is cut at birth. The author is referring to separating from her mother country, Ghana.

to reggae, calypso, high life, jazz, and sometimes R & B, especially Motown songs by Smokey Robinson, Marvin Gaye, or the Supremes. We also listened to country music—Kenny Rogers and Willie Nelson (which might explain my Jimmie Dale Gilmore and Lyle Lovett collections)—and disco. On weekends, my mother—wrapped like a burrito in a single piece of cloth and wearing traditional thong sandals—would listen to Manu Dibango while she was frying fresh fish or dipping a whole chicken she had just killed in our tiny kitchen into a pot of boiling water so its feathers would come off easily; or my father would sit—without shoes, socks, or shirt—in the living room playing Jimmy Cliff and Bob Marley records, his head swaying from side to side, his knees bouncing. Like my mother he, too, was in the company of animals.

On one wall of the living room where he sat and sang was the long, scaly skin of a baby python. On the other was the skinned coat of a wildcat, its head plastered in profile against the white wall, with an oval hole where the eye would have been. Not far from the wildcat were two bows; hanging inside the open arc of each one was a tall, slender pouch containing ten poison-tipped arrows. They were his pride and joy. Sometimes I would beg my father to pull down the arrows and let me touch one. When he did, I would hold it carefully, my small hand trembling as it wrapped itself around the thin stick. After a few minutes, he would take it from me and place it back in its pouch with the other arrows.

I remember asking my father once if he had actually used those very weapons to kill the snake and wildcat. I imagined that only someone with tremendous strength could do something like that—a warrior. I don't recall whether he said yes or no, but the image of my father holding his big, muscular arm high above his head and darting an arrow straight into the body of an animal became my pride and joy. But, like the pig's-feet stew, it was a pride that I was able to acknowledge and partake in only within the confines of our apartment. Most of the exposure I had to homes outside my own was through my friends who invited me over to play or eat dinner. Yet that was all it took for me to see how vastly different the life I led was from their lives. None of the Americans I knew in the suburbs of Washington, D.C., had dead animals and deadly "primitive" weapons tacked up on their walls. They had plaques, awards, framed photos of their smiling families. They had pets, animals that were very much alive and very much loved. They bought their food prepackaged in boxes or in cardboard trays. And there were no bare-chested warriors singing of the Zion train, no mothers peeling, slicing, chopping, killing. Taken out of the context of my home, my life— live chickens, reptile and wildcat skins, bows and arrows—became a source of shame and embarrassment for me.

In this way, the split between the me who lived in that apartment and the me who had to learn how to survive outside it was immediate. It had to be. Initially, I suppose that I viewed that split simply as an external divide, straight and pronounced, like the threshold of our front door, marking the point of separation between two distinct realities. On one side was America, on the other was Ghana. And I didn't know how to bring them together, how to make one make sense *to*, let alone *in*, the other.

Why do you talk like that? Where are you from? Is that string in your hair? Newness is easy to detect, especially with immigrants. Everything about you is a dead giveaway. And people constantly watch and stare through the **scrutinizing**[8] lens of curiosity. That was a foreign thing for me, being questioned, being eyed. From top to bottom, the eyes would travel. From top to bottom,

---

[8] **scrutinizing**—examining; critically peering.

taking a silent inventory of the perceived differences: the way I wore my hair wrapped with thread as thick as an **undiluted**[9] accent, or in small braids intricately woven like a basket atop my head; my clothing, a swirl of bright, festive colors dyed on fabric much too thin for the shivery East Coast climate.

Being black made the transition from Africa to America extremely difficult because it introduced another complex series of boundaries. In a racially divided country, it isn't enough for an immigrant to know how to float in the mainstream. You have to know how to retreat to your margin, where to place your hyphen.[10] You have to know that you are no longer just yourself, you are now an Asian American, a Latin American, an Irish American, or, in my case, a black American. (Only recently has the label become "African American.") At the time of my emigration, the early 1970s, Washington, D.C., a predominantly black city, was awash in a wave of Afrocentricity.[11] Dashikis[12] draped brown shoulders and the black-fisted handle of an Afro pick[13] proudly stuck out in many a back pants pocket. However, despite all the romanticizing and rhetoric about unity and brotherhood, there was a curtain of sheer hostility hanging between black Americans and black Africans.

The black kids I encountered, in and out of school, were the cruelest to me. While other children who were being picked on for whatever trivial or arbitrary reason were called a host of names tailored to their individual inadequacies—Frog Lips, Peanut Head, Four-Eyes, Brace-Face—there was no need to create a name for me.

---

[9] **undiluted**—pure; full-strength; not weakened by the addition of foreign words or sounds.

[10] where to place your hyphen—find yourself among the recognized racial groups. The hyphen the author refers to is the one that connects a given group to the word *American*, as in African-American writers.

[11] Afrocentricity—focus on African roots.

[12] Dashikis—African clothing that became fashionable during the 1970s.

[13] Afro pick—coarse-toothed comb for tending to an Afro hairstyle.

You—you—you African! Go back to Africa! Who I was seemed to be insult enough; where I was from, a horrific place to which one could be banished as a form of punishment.

The white Americans—children and adults—I met attacked me with verbal "kindness," not verbal cruelty. But it was no less hurtful or damaging. Their branding came in the form of adjectives, not nouns—special, exceptional, different, exotic. These words, which flowed so freely from the lips of teachers, parents, and fellow students, were intended to excuse me from my race, to cage me like some zoo animal being domesticated; these words, I realized years later, were intended to absolve those white people from their own racism. I was among the black people to whom many white people were referring when they said, "Some of my best friends. . . ." I was complimented for not talking like "them," not acting like "them," not looking like "them"—"them" being black Americans, the only other physical reflections I had of myself besides my family. But, of course, that wasn't acceptance; it was tolerance.

The one place where I found acceptance was in the company of other immigrants. Together, we concentrated on our similarities, not our differences, because our differences were our similarities. Still, I secretly envied the other foreign kids because I believed that their immigrant experience was somehow more authentic than mine. Unlike me, they were not caught in the racial battlefield of black and white, their *ethnicity* was visible. Mine invariably faded to black. They spoke languages that were identifiable. Everybody's heard of Spanish, Korean, Chinese, even Arabic. The few people who had heard of Ga and Twi colonially labeled them dialects, not languages. Of all the other immigrants, I got along best with my Spanish-speaking friends. For me, they were the middle ground between America and Africa. So when I grew tired of being pendulous, of going to and fro, I entered their culture and it became my home away from home.

In the second grade, I started taking Spanish lessons at my school, and the connection I already felt to that culture was quickly validated. One morning we were learning the Spanish words for breakfast, lunch, dinner, and all the foods usually served during those meals. The teacher, a heavy-hipped Nicaraguan woman with arms that looked like rolling pins, held up a card with a picture of a hazel-colored loaf of bread on it. When she flipped the card over to show us its name in Spanish, the word *pan* was written there in big, bold letters. My jaw dropped in amazement. *Pan* also meant bread in Twi.

One by one, I discovered other words, found other sources of **affirmation**,[14] the biggest being the fact that I had the best of approvals, parental permission, to assimilate into that world. My mum was no stranger to it herself. She did the bulk of her shopping at bodegas,[15] rummaging the shelves for suitable replacements for ingredients needed to prepare customary Ghanaian dishes. Often enough, she would take me along when she went to these stores, where **stodgy**[16] men in blood-smeared aprons would greet us from behind their butcher blocks with smiles and deep-diaphragmed laughter. I felt a sense of freedom in the narrow aisles of those stores, with the tickling smells of hot peppers and the loud chorus of tongues that were kin to my own. I was both outside and inside the split, within the distance between home and here.

But it was not a steady resting place. The Latino kids were also in motion, also trying to reach beyond themselves, searching for their own middle ground. And when I traced the pattern of their movements, it led me

---

[14] **affirmation**—confirmation; proof.

[15] bodegas—specialty grocery stores, especially those with the foods of different ethnic groups.

[16] **stodgy**—old-fashioned; also, thickset, stocky.

right back into my skin. Their middle ground, en route to whiteness—the ultimate immigrant assimilation goal—was black America. So I followed them there. By then, I had befriended two black American **siblings,**[17] Karen and Allen, who lived with their mother in an apartment upstairs from mine. Allen (who is now married to a Ghanaian woman) and I were the same age, but I was closer to Karen, who was a year older. She taught me how to jump double-dutch[18] and "snap" back when kids teased me.

"Tell 'em, 'Yo' momma,'" she'd advise.

"Your mama," I'd repeat, rolling my eyes and sucking my teeth the same as she had done.

Allen would always barge into Karen's room when she was in the midst of schooling me and poke fun. "You sound like a ole white girl," he'd say. And, at that time, that's the last thing I wanted, to "sound" white. I wanted to sound like Karen and Allen and all the other black kids at school. Every day when I left their place and went back to my apartment, I would stand in front of the bathroom mirror and practice speaking like them. I practiced and practiced until, finally, when I listened to the sound of my voice, I could no longer hear an accent. By then, I was in fourth grade.

When I rid myself of my accent, I suddenly internalized the divide, blurred the lines between continents and **allegiances**.[19] There was no middle ground anymore, no threshold, no point of distinction between one reality and another. I had strayed so far away from the place I called my home that I could not find my way back. From that point on, every culture I made contact with seeped in to create one fluid geography within me. Yet as much as I imagined that I could claim them all, I still

---

[17] **siblings**—children who share the same parents; brothers and sisters.

[18] jump double-dutch—jump rope while partners twirl two ropes in opposite directions.

[19] **allegiances**—loyalties.

belonged to none of them. I didn't even belong to the one in which my family resided, the one that had once provided me the safety of a home base. Like everywhere else, I became the "other" there, unable to fully expand and unfold the many selves I now had, unable to ever again feel completely whole.

It seems fitting that, of all the cities I could have chosen to live in when I moved from the city where I grew up, I found myself in Los Angeles. This place is the most accurate external portrait of my internal existence. It is a place where everything is subject to change, where even the land is not stable. It is a city of illusions; what you see is not necessarily what is. People come to Los Angeles in search of their future, in spite of their past. Identities and images are created, killed, or altered here on a daily basis. Over a hundred languages are spoken; cultures overlap, blend, and produce hybrids. There are African-American street vendors selling teriyaki burritos, and Mexican cooks in the kitchens of Jamaican restaurants. Far from being idyllic, it is a city at war with itself, a place where **xenophobia**[20] and self-hatred run rampant. And I have never felt more at peace anywhere else. As the result of a recent incident with my six-year-old daughter, Korama, I began, for the first time, to accept myself, my history of **traversal**.[21] I began to create a context for the cross-cultural life that I have led.

For whatever reason, in the course of one of Korama's kindergarten conversations, she let it be known that my favorite television program is *The X-Files*. That afternoon when I picked her up from school, she told me about the disclosure. "Oh. Okay, Korama," I said, releasing a slight breath of relief. I was happy to know that she and her friends were now exchanging what I believed was less personal information about

---

[20] **xenophobia**—fear of strangers or anything strange or foreign.
[21] **traversal**—passage; crossing.

their parents. Just a few days before, she had spurted out, in a fountain of giggles, that her classmate's mother wore G-strings; and the day before that I learned of another mother's recent miscarriage.

"Mo-o-m," she whined, "it's not okay. They said you like that show because you're an alien. I tried to tell them that you weren't, but Hugo said I was wrong. He said that you're not from America, and that everyone who's not from here is an alien. Is that true? Are you an alien?" She stared at my head as if antennae would pop out at any time. I wasn't sure how to reply, but with the shrewdness that parenthood teaches you, I tried to figure out a way to answer her question without volunteering too much information that might, ultimately, confuse her. While I was mulling it over, she and I walked side by side in silence. With each step, I felt a distance growing between us. It was a distance much wider than the gap of generations that eventually settles between parents and children. And it was haunting.

For a moment, her stare was as disempowering as those of the American children whom I had encountered as a child, her questions as offensive. I wanted to arm myself against the pain of being reminded that I was "other." I wanted to beg that little girl before me to try, to just try to accept—if not love—me for who I was, the way I was, no matter how different that seemed from the way she was. But I knew I didn't have to, because she already did. "Yes," I finally said to Korama, "I am." I explained to her that in addition to creatures from outer space, the word "alien" was used to refer to human beings from other countries. I expected her to be a bit confused, but she didn't appear to be. She nodded, reached out for my hand as we approached the street we had to cross to get to our apartment, and the distance disappeared.

When I tucked her into bed that evening, she raised the subject again. "Mom, will you always be an alien?"

she asked. And, again, I tried to find a straightforward, uncomplicated response, this time to a question I had been trying unsuccessfully to answer for over twenty years. "No," I told her. "Not if I become an American." Up until the second I said that, I had never so much as considered becoming a United States citizen. In the belief that I would one day return to the country of my birth, I had never made a commitment to being in the country where I have spent the better part of my life. I had always thought of naturalization as nothing more than a piece of paper one received after passing a test, a series of questions designed to assess one's technical knowledge of the country and the laws by which it is governed. If that's the case, I could live or die without that slip of paper, that change of nationality. It wouldn't make a difference one way or the other. I have lived my life as an alien, an outsider trying to find a way and a place to fit in. And it is only through that experience that I have come to think of myself not as a citizen of one country or another but, rather, of an entire world.

QUESTIONS TO CONSIDER

1. How is the author's experiment with a vegetarian diet a reflection of her "half and half" status?

2. In what ways is the author's childhood home in Washington, D.C., different from her friends' homes? In what ways is it similar?

3. What does the author mean when she says that being told she wasn't like other black Americans "wasn't acceptance; it was tolerance"? What is the difference between acceptance and tolerance?

4. How did the conversation with her daughter, Korama, help bring peace of mind to the author?

Address to the United Farm Workers of America

BY CESAR CHAVEZ

By the mid-twentieth century, many Latinos, both legal and illegal immigrants, were working for low wages in farm fields across the country. They are known as "migrant workers" because they follow the harvest from one area of the country to another. For more than two decades, beginning in the 1960s, Cesar Chavez, president of the United Farm Workers of America, led a movement to improve conditions for migrant farm workers. He gained national attention through his successful appeal to the public to boycott lettuce and grapes because of the growers' hiring practices. In this excerpt from a speech he gave in California on November 9, 1984, Chavez shares his vision of an empowered Latino population in the United States and relates his work to his own experiences as a child in a family of migrant farm workers in California.

Twenty-one years ago last September, on a lonely stretch of railroad track paralleling U.S. Highway 101 near Salinas, 32 Bracero farm workers lost their lives in a tragic accident.

The Braceros had been imported from Mexico to work on California farms. They died when their bus, which was converted from a flatbed track, drove in front of a freight train.

Conversion of the bus had not been approved by any government agency. The driver had "tunnel" vision.

Most of the bodies lay unidentified for days. No one, including the grower who employed the workers, even knew their names.

Today, thousands of farm workers live under savage conditions—beneath trees and amid garbage and human excrement—near tomato fields in San Diego County, tomato fields which use the most modern farm technology.

Vicious rats gnaw on them as they sleep. They walk miles to buy food at inflated prices. And they carry in water from irrigation pumps.

Child labor is still common in many farm areas.

As much as 30 percent of Northern California's garlic harvesters are under-aged children. Kids as young as six years old have voted in state-conducted union elections since they qualified as workers.

Some 800,000 under-aged children work with their families harvesting crops across America. Babies born to migrant workers suffer 25 percent higher infant mortality than the rest of the population.

Malnutrition among migrant worker children is 10 times higher than the national rate.

Farm workers' average life expectancy is still 49 years—compared to 73 years for the average American.

All my life, I have been driven by one dream, one goal, one vision: To overthrow a farm labor system in this nation which treats farm workers as if they were not important human beings.

Farm workers are not agricultural implements. They are not beasts of burden—to be used and discarded.

That dream was born in my youth. It was nurtured in my early days of organizing. It has flourished. It has been attacked.

I'm not very different from anyone else who has ever tried to accomplish something with his life. My motivation comes from my personal life—from watching what my mother and father went through when I was growing up; from what we experienced as migrant farm workers in California.

That dream, that vision, grew from my own experience with racism, with hope, with the desire to be treated fairly and to see my people treated as human beings and not as **chattel**.[1]

It grew from anger and rage—emotions I felt 40 years ago when people of my color were denied the right to see a movie or eat at a restaurant in many parts of California.

It grew from the frustration and humiliation I felt as a boy who couldn't understand how the growers could abuse and exploit farm workers when there were so many of us and so few of them.

Later, in the '50s, I experienced a different kind of exploitation. In San Jose, in Los Angeles and in other urban communities, we—the Mexican American people—were dominated by a majority that was Anglo.[2]

I began to realize what other minority people had discovered: That the only answer—the only hope—was in organizing. More of us had to become citizens. We had to register to vote. And people like me had to develop the skills it would take to organize, to educate, to help empower the Chicano[3] people.

---

[1] **chattel**—property, that is, slaves.

[2] Anglo—people of English heritage; white North Americans not of Hispanic or French descent.

[3] Chicano—a term for persons of Mexican descent commonly used during the 1980s.

I spent many years—before we founded the union—learning how to work with people.

We experienced some successes in voter registration, in politics, in battling racial discrimination—successes in an era when Black Americans were just beginning to assert their civil rights and when political awareness among Hispanics was almost non-existent.

But deep in my heart, I knew I could never be happy unless I tried organizing the farm workers. I didn't know if I would succeed. But I had to try.

All Hispanics[4]—urban and rural, young and old—are connected to the farm workers' experience. We had all lived through the fields—or our parents had. We shared that common humiliation.

How could we progress as a people, even if we lived in the cities, while the farm workers—men and women of our color—were condemned to a life without pride?

How could we progress as a people while the farm workers—who symbolized our history in this land—were denied self-respect?

How could our people believe that their children could become lawyers and doctors and judges and business people while this shame, this injustice was permitted to continue?

Those who attack our union often say, "It's not really a union, it's something else: A social movement. A civil rights movement. It's something dangerous."

They're half right. The United Farm Workers is first and foremost a union. A union like any other. A union that either produces for its members on the bread and butter issues or doesn't survive.

But the UFW has always been something more than a union—although it's never been dangerous if you believe in the Bill of Rights.

---

[4] Hispanics—people of Spanish-speaking heritage, including Mexicans.

The UFW was the beginning! We attacked that historical source of shame and infamy that our people in this country lived with. We attacked that injustice, not by complaining; not by seeking hand-outs; not by becoming soldiers in the War on Poverty.

We organized!

Farm workers acknowledged we had allowed ourselves to become victims in a democratic society—a society where majority rule and collective bargaining are supposed to be more than academic theories or **political rhetoric**.[5] And by addressing this historical problem, we created confidence and pride and hope in an entire people's ability to create the future.

The UFW's survival—its existence—was not in doubt in my mind when the time began to come—after the union became visible—when Chicanos started entering college in greater numbers, when Hispanics began running for public office in greater numbers—when our people started asserting their rights on a broad range of issues and in many communities across the country.

The union's survival—its very existence—sent out a signal to all Hispanics that we were fighting for our dignity, that we were challenging and overcoming injustice, that we were empowering the least educated among us—the poorest among us.

The message was clear: If it could happen in the fields, it could happen anywhere—in the cities, in the courts, in the city councils, in the state legislatures.

I didn't really appreciate it at the time, but the coming of our union signaled the start of great changes among Hispanics that are only now beginning to be seen.

I've traveled to every part of this nation. I have met and spoken with thousands of Hispanics from every walk of life—from every social and economic class.

---

[5] **political rhetoric**—insincere promises from politicians.

One thing I hear most often from Hispanics, regardless of age or position—and from many non-Hispanics as well, is that the farm workers gave them hope that they could succeed and the inspiration to work for change. . . .

And Hispanics across California and the nation who don't work in agriculture are better off today because of what the farm workers taught people about organization, about pride and strength, about seizing control over their own lives.

Tens of thousands of the children and grandchildren of farm workers and the children and grandchildren of poor Hispanics are moving out of the fields and out of the *barrios*[6]—and into the professions and into business and into politics. And that movement cannot be reversed!

Our union will forever exist as an empowering force among Chicanos in the Southwest. And that means our power and our influence will grow and not diminish.

Two major trends give us hope and encouragement.

First, our union has returned to a tried and tested weapon in the farm workers' non-violent arsenal—the boycott!

After the Agricultural Labor Relations Act became law in California in 1975, we dismantled our boycott to work with the law.

During the early- and mid-'70s, millions of Americans supported our boycotts. After 1975, we redirected our efforts from the boycott to organizing and winning elections under the law.

The law helped farm workers make progress in overcoming poverty and injustice. At companies where farm workers are protected by union contracts, we have made progress in overcoming child labor, in overcoming miserable wages and working conditions, in overcoming sexual harassment of women workers,

---

[6] *barrios*—Spanish-speaking neighborhoods.

in overcoming dangerous pesticides which poison our people and poison the food we all eat.

Where we have organized, these injustices soon pass into history. . . .

The Louis Harris poll revealed that 17 million American adults boycotted grapes. We are convinced that those people and that good will have not disappeared.

That segment of the population which makes our boycotts work are the Hispanics, the Blacks, the other minorities and our allies in labor and the church. But it is also an entire generation of young Americans who matured politically and socially in the 1960's and '70s— millions of people for whom boycotting grapes and other products became a socially accepted pattern of behavior.

If you were young, Anglo and on or near campus during the late '60s and early '70s, chances are you supported farm workers.

Fifteen years later, the men and women of that generation are alive and well. They are in their mid-30s and '40s. They are pursuing professional careers. Their disposable income is relatively high. But they are still inclined to respond to an appeal from farm workers. The union's mission still has meaning for them.

Only today we must translate the importance of a union for farm workers into the language of the 1980s. Instead of talking about the right to organize, we must talk about protection against sexual harassment in the fields. We must speak about the right to quality food— and food that is safe to eat.

I can tell you that the new language is working; the 17 million are still there. They are responding—not to picketlines and leafletting[7] alone, but to the high-tech boycott of today—a boycott that uses computers and direct mail and advertising techniques which have revolutionized business and politics in recent years.

---

[7] leafletting—distributing persuasive literature.

We have achieved more success with the boycott in the first 11 months of 1984 than we achieved in the 14 years since 1970.

The other trend that gives us hope is the monumental growth of Hispanic influence in this country and what that means in increased population, increased social and economic clout, and increased political influence.

South of the Sacramento River in California, Hispanics now make up more than 25 percent of the population. That figure will top 30 percent by the year 2000.

There are 1.1 million Spanish-surnamed registered voters in California; 85 percent are Democrats; only 13 percent are Republicans.

In 1975, there were 200 Hispanic elected officials at all levels of government. In 1984, there are over 400 elected judges, city council members, mayors and legislators.

In light of these trends, it is absurd to believe or suggest that we are going to go back in time—as a union or as a people!

The growers often try to blame the union for their problems—to lay their sins off on us—sins for which they only have themselves to blame.

The growers only have themselves to blame as they begin to reap the harvest from decades of environmental damage they have brought upon the land—the pesticides, the herbicides, the soil fumigants,[8] the fertilizers, the salt deposits from thoughtless irrigation—the ravages from years of unrestrained poisoning of our soil and water.

Thousands of acres of land in California have already been **irrevocably**[9] damaged by this **wanton**[10] abuse of nature. Thousands more will be lost unless growers understand that dumping more poisons on the soil won't solve their problems—in the short term or the long term.

---

[8] fumigants—gaseous poisons sprayed on farms to kill pests.

[9] **irrevocably**—in a way that cannot be taken back.

[10] **wanton**—immoral.

Health authorities in many San Joaquin Valley towns already warn young children and pregnant women not to drink the water because of nitrates from fertilizers which have contaminated the groundwater.

The growers only have themselves to blame for an increasing demand by consumers for higher quality food—food that isn't tainted by toxics; food that doesn't result from plant mutations or chemicals which produce red, luscious-looking tomatoes—that taste like alfalfa.

The growers are making the same mistake American automakers made in the '60s and '70s when they refused to produce small economical cars—and opened the door to increased foreign competition.

Growers only have themselves to blame for increasing attacks on their publicly financed hand-outs and government welfare: Water subsidies; mechanization research; huge subsidies for not growing crops.

These special privileges came into being before the Supreme Court's one-person, one-vote decision—a time when rural lawmakers dominated the Legislature and the Congress. Soon, those hand-outs could be in jeopardy as government searches for more revenue and as urban taxpayers take a closer look at farm programs—and who they really benefit.

The growers only have themselves to blame for the humiliation they have brought upon succeeding waves of immigrant groups which have sweated and sacrificed for 100 years to make this industry rich. For generations, they have **subjugated**[11] entire races of dark-skinned farm workers.

These are the sins of the growers, not the farm workers. We didn't poison the land. We didn't open the door to imported produce. We didn't covet billions of dollars in government hand-outs. We didn't abuse and exploit the people who work the land.

---

[11] **subjugated**—conquered; controlled; enslaved.

Today, the growers are like a punch-drunk old boxer who doesn't know he's past his prime. The times are changing. The political and social environment has changed. The chickens are coming home to roost—and the time to account for past sins is approaching. . . .

History and inevitability are on our side. The farm workers and their children—and the Hispanics and their children—are the future in California. And corporate growers are the past! . . .

Once social change begins, it cannot be reversed.

You cannot uneducate the person who has learned to read. You cannot humiliate the person who feels pride. You cannot oppress the people who are not afraid anymore.

Our opponents must understand that it's not just a union we have built. Unions, like other institutions, can come and go.

But we're more than an institution. For nearly 20 years, our union has been on the cutting edge of a people's cause—and you cannot do away with an entire people; you cannot stamp out a people's cause.

Regardless of what the future holds for the union, regardless of what the future holds for farm workers, our accomplishments cannot be undone. "La Causa"—our cause—doesn't have to be experienced twice.

The consciousness and pride that were raised by our union are alive and thriving inside millions of young Hispanics who will never work on a farm!

Like the other immigrant groups, the day will come when we win the economic and political rewards which are in keeping with our numbers in society. The day will come when the politicians do the right thing by our people out of political necessity and not out of charity or idealism.

That day may not come this year. That day may not come during this decade. But it will come, someday!

And when that day comes, we shall see the fulfillment of that passage from the Book of Matthew in the New Testament, "That the last shall be first and the first shall be last."

And on that day, our nation shall fulfill its creed—and that fulfillment shall enrich us all.

QUESTIONS TO CONSIDER

1. How did the experiences of his childhood shape Chavez's commitment to his cause?

2. How, according to Chavez, does the farm workers' experience and the UFW represent all Latinos?

3. Why do you think Cesar Chavez is among the most revered Latino leaders of recent times?

Immigrant
Stories

part
four

In the Gateway of Nations

BY JACOB A. RIIS

Between Jacob Riis's arrival from Denmark in 1870 and the time he wrote this article for The Century Magazine *in 1903, the nature of immigration to the United States had changed dramatically. By 1903, the proportion of southern and eastern Europeans coming through the federal immigration station at Ellis Island in New York City's harbor had sharply increased. Despite the worries and criticisms of his fellow citizens, crusading journalist and reformer Riis expressed his belief that American institutions would absorb these newcomers successfully.*

How it all came back to me; that Sunday in early June when I stood, a lonely immigrant lad, at the steamer's rail and looked out upon the New World of my dreams; upon the life that **teemed**[1] ashore and afloat, and was all so strange; upon the miles of streets that led nowhere I knew of; upon the sunlit harbor, and the gay

---

[1] **teemed**—poured out.

excursion-boats that went to and fro with their careless crowds; upon the green hills of Brooklyn; upon the majestic sweep of the lordly river. I thought that I had never seen anything so beautiful, and I think so now, after more than thirty years, when I come into New York's harbor on a steamer. But now I am coming home; then all the memories lay behind. I squared my shoulders against what was coming. I was ready and eager. But for a passing moment, there at the rail, I would have given it all for one familiar face, one voice I knew.

How it all came back as I stood on the deck of the ferry-boat plowing its way from the Battery Park to Ellis Island. They were there, my fellow-travelers of old: the men with their strange burdens of feather beds, cooking-pots, and things unknowable, but mighty of bulk in bags of bed-ticking[2] much the worse for wear. There was the very fellow with the knapsack that had never left him once on the way over, not even when he slept. Then he used it as a pillow. It was when he ate that we got fleeting glimpses of its interminable coils of sausage, its uncanny depths of pumpernickel and cheese that **eked**[3] out the steamer's fare. I saw him last in Pittsburg, still with his sack. What long-forgotten memories that crowd stirred! The women were there, with their gaudy head-dresses and big gold ear-rings. But their hair was raven black instead of yellow, and on the young girl's cheek there was a richer hue than the pink and white I knew. The men, too, looked like swarthy gnomes[4] compared with the stalwart Swede or German of my day. They were the same, and yet not the same. I glanced out over the bay, and behold! all things were changed. For the wide stretch of squat houses pierced by the single spire of Trinity Church there had come a sky-line of towering battlements, in the shelter of which nestled Castle

---

[2] bed-ticking—mattress stuffing.

[3] **eked**—supplemented.

[4] swarthy gnomes—dark complexioned dwarfs.

Garden, once more a popular pleasure resort. My eye rested upon one copper-roofed palace, and I recalled with a smile my first errand ashore to a barber's shop in the old Washington Inn, that stood where it is built. I went to get a bath and to have my hair cut, and they charged me two dollars in gold for it, with gold at a big premium; which charge, when I objected to it, was adjudged fair by a man who said he was a notary—an office I was given to understand was equal in dignity to that of a justice of peace or of the Supreme Court. And when, still unawed, I appealed to the policeman outside, that **functionary**[5] heard me through, dangling his club from his thumb, and delivered himself of a weary "G'wan, now!" that ended it. There was no more.

"For the loikes o' them!" I turned sharply to the voice at my elbow, and caught the ghost of a grimace on the face of the old apple-woman who sat disdainfully dealing out bananas to the "Dagos" and "sheenies" of her untamed prejudices, sole survival in that crowd of the day that was past. No, not quite the only one. I was another. She recognized it with a look and a nod.

A curiously changing procession has passed through Uncle Sam's gateway since I stood at the steamer's rail that June morning in the long ago. Then the tide of Teutonic[6] immigration that peopled the great Northwest was still rising. The last herd of buffaloes had not yet gone over the divide before the white-tented prairie-schooner's[7] advance; the battle of the Little Big Horn was yet unfought. A circle drawn on the map of Europe around the countries smitten with the America-unrest would, even a dozen years later than that, have had Paris for its center. "To-day," said Assistant Commissioner of Immigration McSweeney, speaking before the National Geographic Society last winter, "a circle of the same size,

---

[5] **functionary**—officer.

[6] Teutonic—German.

[7] prairie-schooner's—covered wagon's.

including the sources of the present immigration to the United States, would have its center in Constantinople."[8] And he pointed out that as steamboat transportation developed on the Danube the center would be more firmly fixed in the East, where whole populations, notably in the Balkan States,[9] are catching the infection or having it thrust upon them. Secretary Hay's recent note to the powers in defense of the Rumanian Jews told part of that story. Even the Italian, whose country sent us half a million immigrants in the last four years, may then have to yield first place to the hill men with whom kidnapping is an established industry. I mean no disrespect to their Sicilian brother bandit. With him it is a fine art.

While the statesman ponders the perils of unrestricted immigration, and debates with organized labor whom to shut out and how, the procession moves serenely on. Ellis Island is the nation's gateway to the promised land. There is not another such to be found anywhere. In a single day it has handled seven thousand immigrants. "Handled" is the word; nothing short of it will do.

"How much you got?" shouts the inspector at the head of the long file moving up from the **quay**[10] between iron rails, and, remembering, in the same breath shrieks out, "Quanto moneta?" with a gesture that brings up from the depths of Pietro's pocket a pitiful handful of paper money. Before he has it half out, the interpreter has him by the wrist, and with a quick movement shakes the bills out upon the desk as a dice-thrower "chucks" the ivories.

Ten, twenty, forty lire. He shakes his head. Not much, but—he glances at the ship's manifest[11]—is he going to friends?

---

[8] Constantinople—capital of the Byzantine Empire, now Istanbul, the capital of Turkey.

[9] Balkan States—countries in eastern Europe around the Balkan peninsula, Montenegro, Serbia, Albania, Bosnia, Bulgaria, continental Greece, European Turkey, and Yugoslavia.

[10] **quay**—wharf.

[11] manifest—itemized list of a ship's cargo.

"Si, si! signor," says Pietro, eagerly; his brother of the vineyard—oh, a fine vineyard! And he holds up a bundle of grapesticks in evidence. He has brought them all the way from the village at home to set them out in his brother's field.

"Ugh," grunts the inspector as he stuffs the money back in the man's pocket, shoves him on, and yells, "Wie viel geld?"[12] at a hapless German next in line. "They won't grow. They never do. Bring 'em just the same." By which time the German has joined Pietro in his bewilderment en route for something or somewhere, shoved on by guards, and the inspector wrestles with a "case" who is trying to sneak in on false pretenses. No go; he is hauled by an officer and ticketed "S.I.," printed large on a conspicuous card. It means that he is held for the Board of Special Inquiry, which will sift his story. Before they reach the door there is an outcry and a scuffle. The tide has turned against the Italian and the steamship company. He was detected throwing the card, back up, under the heater, hoping to escape in the crowd. He will have to go back. An eagle eye, with a memory that never lets go, has spotted him as once before deported. King Victor Emmanuel[13] has achieved a reluctant subject; Uncle Sam has lost a citizen. Which is the better off?

A **stalwart**[14] Montenegrin comes next, lugging his gun of many an ancient feud, and proves his title clear. Neither the feud nor the blunderbuss[15] is dangerous under the American sun; they will both seem grotesque before he has been here a month. A Syrian from Mount Lebanon holds up the line while the inspector fires questions at him which it is not given to the uninitiated ear to make out. Goodness knows where they get it all. There seems to be no language or dialect under the sun that does not lie handy to the tongue of these men at the

---

[12] Wie viel geld?—How much money (do you have)?

[13] King Victor Emmanuel—king of Italy 1900–1945.

[14] stalwart—strong; stout.

[15] blunderbuss—kind of gun.

desk. There are twelve of them. One would never dream there were twelve such linguists in the country till he hears them and sees them; for half their talk is done with their hands and shoulders and with the official steel pen that transfixes an object of suspicion like a merciless spear, upon the point of which it writhes in vain. The Syrian wriggles off by good luck, and to-morrow will be peddling "holy earth from Jerusalem," **purloined**[16] on his way through the Battery,[17] at half a dollar a clod. He represents the purely commercial element of our immigration, and represents it well—or ill, as you take it. He cares neither for land and cattle, nor for freedom to worship or work, but for cash in the way of trade. And he gets it. Hence more come every year.

Looking down upon the crowd in the gateway, jostling, bewildered, and **voluble**[18] in a thousand tongues—so at least it sounds,—it seems like a hopeless mass of confusion. As a matter of fact, it is all order and perfect system, begun while the steamer was yet far out at sea. By the time the lighters are tied up at the Ellis Island wharf their human cargo is numbered and lettered in groups that correspond with like entries in the manifest, and so are marshaled upon and over the bridge that leads straight into the United States to the man with the pen who asks questions. When the crowd is great and pressing, they camp by squads in little stalls bearing their **proprietary**[19] stamp, as it were, finding one another and being found when astray by the mystic letter that brings together in the close companionship of a common peril—the pen, one stroke which can shut the gate against them—men and women who in another hour go their way, very likely never to meet or hear of one

---

[16] **purloined**—stolen.

[17] the Battery—a section of New York City at the southern tip of Manhattan Island.

[18] **voluble**—fluent; speaking easily.

[19] **proprietary**—exclusively owned; private.

another again on earth. The sense of the impending trial sits visibly upon the waiting crowd. Here and there a masterful spirit strides boldly on; the mass huddle close, with more or less anxious look. Five minutes after it is over, eating their dinner in the big waiting-room, they present an entirely different appearance. Signs and numbers have disappeared. The groups are recasting themselves on lines of nationality and personal preference. Care is cast to the winds. A look of serene contentment sits upon the face that gropes among the **hieroglyphics**[20] on the lunch-counter bulletin-board for the things that pertain to him and his:

Röget Fisk[21]

Kielbasa[22]

Szynka Gotowana[23]

"Ugh!" says my companion, home-bred on fried meat, "I wouldn't eat it." No more would I if it tastes as it reads; but then, there is no telling. That lunch-counter is not half bad. From the kosher sausage to the big red apples that stare at one—at the children especially— wherever one goes, it is really very appetizing. The *röget fisk* I know about; it is good.

The women guard the baggage in their seats while *pater familias*[24] takes a look around. Half of them munch their New World sandwich with an I-care-not-what-comes-next-the-worst-is-over air; the other half scribble elaborately with stubby pencils on postal cards that are all star-spangled and striped with white and red. It is their announcement to those waiting at home that they have passed the gate and are within.

Behind carefully guarded doors wait the "outs," the detained immigrants, for the word that will let down the

---

[20] **hieroglyphics**—writing that uses pictorial symbols.

[21] Röget Fisk—Norwegian fish dish.

[22] Kielbasa—Polish sausage.

[23] Szynka Gotowana—Polish pork dish.

[24] *pater familias*—(Latin) the male head of the household.

bars or fix them in place immovably. The guard is for a double purpose: that no one shall leave or enter the detention—"pen" it used to be called; but the new regime under President Roosevelt's[25] commission has set its face sternly against the term. The law of kindness rules on Ellis Island; a note posted conspicuously invites every employee who cannot fall in with it to get out as speedily as he may. So now it is the detention-"room" into which no outsider with unfathomed intentions may enter. Here are the old, the stricken, waiting for friends able to keep them; the pitiful little colony of women without the shield of a man's name in the hour of their greatest need; the young and pretty and thoughtless, for whom one sends up a silent prayer of thanksgiving at the thought of the mob at that other gate, in Battery Park, beyond which Uncle Sam's strong hand reaches not to guide or guard. And the hopelessly bewildered are there, often enough exasperated at the restraint, which they cannot understand. The law of kindness is put to a severe strain here by ignorance and stubbornness. In it all they seem, some of them, to be able to make out only that their personal liberty, their "rights," are interfered with. How quickly they sprout in the gateway! This German girl who is going to her uncle flatly refuses to send him word that she is here. She has been taught to look out for sharpers[26] and to guard her little store well, and detects in the telegraph toll a scheme to rob her of one of her cherished silver marks. To all reasoning she turns a deaf and defiant ear: he will find her. The important thing is that she is here. That her uncle is in Newark makes no impression on her. Is it not all America?

A name is cried at the door, and there is a rush. Angelo, whose destination, repeated with joyful **volubility**[27] in

---

[25] President Roosevelt's—of Theodore Roosevelt, president of the United States from 1901 to 1913.

[26] sharpers—tricksters; cheaters.

[27] **volubility**—fluency.

every key and accent, puzzled the officials for a time, is going. His hour of deliverance has come. "Pringvilliamas" yielded to patient scrutiny at last. It was "Springfield, Mass.," and impatient friends are waiting for Angelo up there. His countryman, who is going to his brother-in-law, but has "forgotten his American name," takes leave of him wistfully. He is penniless, and near enough the "age limit of adaptability"[28] to be an object of doubt and deliberation.

In laying down that limit, as in the case of the other that fixes the amount of money in hand to prove the immigrant's title to enter, the island is a law unto itself. Under the folds of the big flag which drapes the tribunal of the Board of Special Inquiry, claims from every land under the sun are weighed and adjusted. It is ever a matter of individual consideration. A man without a cent, but with a pair of strong hands and with a head that sits firmly on rugged shoulders, might be better material for citizenship in every way than Mr. Moneybags with no other recommendation; and to shut out an aged father and mother for whom the children are able and willing to care would be inhuman. The gist of the thing was put clearly in President Roosevelt's message in the reference to a certain economic standard of fitness for citizenship that must govern, and does govern, the keepers of the gate. Into it enter not only the man's years and his pocketbook, but the whole man, and he himself virtually decides the case. Not many, I fancy, are sent back without good cause. The law of kindness is strained, if anything, in favor of the immigrant to the doubtful advantage of Uncle Sam, on the presumption, I suppose, that he can stand it.

But at the locked door of the rejected, those whom the Board has heard and shut out, the process stops short. At least, it did when I was there. I stopped it. It was when the attendant pointed out an ex-bandit, a black and surly

---

[28] "age limit of adaptability"—almost too old to adapt to a new life.

fellow with the strength of a wild boar, who was wanted on the other side for sticking a knife into a man. The knife they had taken from him here was the central exhibit in a shuddering array of such which the doorkeeper kept in his corner. That morning the bandit had "soaked" a countryman of his, waiting to be deported for the debility of old age. I could not help it. "I hope you—" I began, and stopped short, remembering the "notice" on the wall. But the man at the door understood. "I did," he nodded. "I soaked him a couple." And I felt better. I confess it, and I will not go back to the island, if Commissioner Williams will not let me, for breaking his law.

But I think he will, for within the hour I saw him himself "soak" a Flemish peasant twice his size for beating and abusing a child. The man turned and towered above the commissioner with angry looks, but the ordinarily quiet little man presented so suddenly a fierce and warlike aspect that, though neither understood a word of what the other said, the case was made clear to the brute on the instant, and he slunk away. Commissioner William's law of kindness is all right. It is based upon the correct observation that not one in a thousand of those who land at Ellis Island needs harsh treatment, but advice and help—which does not prevent the thousandth case from receiving its full due.

QUESTIONS TO CONSIDER

1. In what ways did immigration to the United States change between the time when Riis was a boy (the late 1870s) and 1903, the year that the article was written?

2. What was the process that immigrants endured at "Uncle Sam's gateway," Ellis Island? What criteria determined whether they stayed or were sent back?

3. How do you think Riis feels about the "new" immigrants? Explain.

Living in America

▲

Riis portrait Photographer Jacob Riis emigrated to the United States from Denmark in 1870. After years of extreme poverty and hardship he finally found employment as a police reporter for the *New York Tribune* in 1877. In the 1880s he crusaded for better living conditions for the thousands of immigrants flocking to New York in search of new opportunities.

▲

Hester Street American city streets filled with the foreign tongues and cooking smells of Europe. Riis captured on film this scene of Hester Street in the Jewish ghetto of New York City in the 1890s.

Low-life Dive Those who had nowhere else to go found a home in unauthorized lodgings like this one. Lodgers paid five cents to sleep anywhere they could find a spot in the crowded tenements.

▼

▲

Lacemakers in Tenement Mrs. Vencique and her fifteen-year-old sister make lace collars in the kitchen of their tenement in 1911. Mrs. Vencique's baby sleeps on her lap.

◀ **Mill Workers** Among these men are four boys who worked in a mill in Lowell, Massachusetts, in 1911. Immigrant children worked in mills or factories to help support their families.

Japanese Being Vaccinated Japanese immigrants are vaccinated on board a Pacific steamship bound for Hawaii in 1904. Immigrants were often vaccinated to prevent them from spreading disease in America.
▼

▲

Immigrants with Shadows
"They would close to the new-comer the bridge that carried their fathers over" proclaims this 1893 *Puck* cartoon. Ironically, the settled population of previous immigrants often worked hard to keep new immigrants out.

Liberty Protecting the Chinese This cartoon by famous political cartoonist Thomas Nast shows the figure of Liberty protecting a Chinese immigrant seated in front of a wall emblazoned with racial slurs. ▶

Anti-German Sentiment During World War I Expressing a popular view of German Americans, W.A. Rogers's 1918 cartoon shows Uncle Sam glaring at an "enemy alien" who crowds him on a bench in "Liberty Park."

▼

from

The Jungle

BY UPTON SINCLAIR

*In 1904, a muckraking journalist named Upton Sinclair visited
Chicago to do research for a novel exposing the truth about the
meatpacking industry. For seven weeks, he lived in a neighborhood
called Packingtown near the stockyards. There he interviewed workers,
lawyers, doctors, saloonkeepers, and social workers. The result was
one of the most famous of all immigrant stories, The Jungle. This
classic exposé led to the first national government regulations on
the purity of food but did not inspire public outrage concerning
the plight of immigrant workers in American factories. Sinclair had
intended his work to show "the breaking of human hearts by a
system which exploits the labor of men and women for profit."
Surprised by the public reaction, he wrote, "I aimed at the public's
heart and by accident I hit it in the stomach." In the selection
given here, Jurgis Rudkus, newly arrived from Poland, learns of
some of the horrors in the plants. Like many other immigrants,
Jurgis had little choice but to take the lowest-paying, least desirable
job available.*

Then one Sunday evening, Jurgis sat puffing his pipe by the kitchen stove, and talking with an old fellow whom Jonas had introduced, and who worked in the canning rooms at Durham's [a meat-packing company]; and so Jurgis learned a few things about the great and only Durham canned goods, which had become a national institution. They were regular alchemists[1] at Durham's; they advertised a mushroom catsup, and the men who made it did not know what a mushroom looked like. They advertised "potted chicken,"—and it was like the boarding house soup of the comic papers, through which a chicken had walked with rubbers on. Perhaps they had a secret process for making chickens chemically—who knows? said Jurgis's friend; the things that went into the mixture were tripe,[2] and the fat of pork, and beef suet,[3] and hearts of beef, and finally the waste ends of veal, when they had any. They put these up in several grades, and sold them at several prices; but the contents of the cans all came out of the same hopper. And then there was the "potted game" and "potted grouse," "potted ham" and "deviled ham"—de-vyled, as the men called it. "De-vyled" ham was made out of the waste ends of smoked beef that were too small to be sliced by the machines; and also tripe, dyed with chemicals so that it would not show white; and trimmings of hams and corned beef; and potatoes, skins and all; and finally the hard cartilaginous gullets[4] of beef, after the tongues had been cut out. All this **ingenious**[5] mixture was ground up and flavored with spice to make it taste like something. Anybody who could invent a new imitation had been sure of a fortune from old Durham, said

---

[1] alchemists—chemists of the Middle Ages who tried to turn base metals into gold.

[2] tripe—meat from the walls of the stomachs of cattle.

[3] suet—meat from the hard fat from around the kidney and loins.

[4] cartilaginous gullets—tough, connective tissues in the throats of cattle.

[5] **ingenious**—clever; imaginative.

Jurgis' informant; but it was hard to think of anything new in a place where so many sharp wits had been at work for so long; where men welcomed tuberculosis in the cattle they were feeding, because it made them fatten more quickly; and where they bought up all the **rancid**[6] old butter left over in the grocery stores of a continent, and "oxidized" it by a forced-air process, to take away the odor, rechurned it with skim-milk, and sold it in bricks in the cities! Up to a year or two ago it had been the custom to kill horses in the yards—ostensibly for fertilizer; but after long agitation the newspapers had been able to make the public realize that the horses were being canned. Now it was against the law to kill horses in Packingtown, and the law was really complied with—for the present at any rate. Any day, however, one might see sharp-horned and shaggy-haired creatures running with the sheep—and yet what a job you would have to get the public to believe that a good part of what it buys for lamb and mutton is really goat's flesh!

There was another interesting set of statistics that a person might have gathered in Packingtown—those of the various afflictions of the workers. When Jurgis had first inspected the packing-plants with the Szedvilas, he had marveled while he listened to the tales of all the things that were made out of the carcasses of animals, and of the lesser industries that were maintained there; now he found that each one of these lesser industries was a separate little inferno, in its way as horrible as the killing-beds, the source and fountain of them all. The workers in each of them had their own particular diseases. And the wandering visitor might be skeptical about all the swindles, but he could not be skeptical about these, for the worker bore the evidence of them about on his own person—generally he had only to hold out his hand.

---

[6] **rancid**—spoiled-smelling.

There were the men in the pickle-rooms, for instance, where old Antanas had gotten his death; scarce one of these that had not some spot of horror on his person. Let a man so much as scrape his finger pushing a truck in the pickle-rooms, and he might have a sore that would put him out of the world; all the joints in his fingers might be eaten by the acid, one by one. Of the butchers and floorsmen, the boners and beeftrimmers, and all those who used knives, you could scarcely find a person who had the use of his thumb; time and time again the base of it had been slashed, till it was a mere lump of flesh against which the man pressed the knife to hold it. The hands of these men would be criss-crossed with cuts, until you could no longer pretend to count them or to trace them. They would have no nails,—they had worn them off pulling hides; their knuckles were swollen so that their fingers spread out like a fan. There were men who worked in the cooking-rooms, in the midst of steam and sickening odors, by artificial light; in these rooms the germs of tuberculosis might live for two years, but the supply was renewed every hour. There were the beef-luggers, who carried two-hundred pound quarters into the refrigerator-cars; a fearful kind of work, that began at four o'clock in the morning, and that wore out the most powerful men in a few years. There were those who worked in the chilling-rooms and whose special disease was rheumatism;[7] the time-limit that a man could work in the chilling-rooms was said to be five years. There were the wool pluckers, whose hands went to pieces even sooner than the hands of the pickle-men; for the pelts of the sheep had to be painted with acid to loosen the wool, and then the pluckers had to pull out this wool with their bare hands, till the acid had eaten their fingers off. There were those who made tins for the canned-meat; and their hands, too, were a maze of cuts,

---

[7] rheumatism—crippling disease of the muscles and joints.

and each cut represented a chance for blood-poisoning. Some worked at the stamping machines, and it was very seldom that one could work there long at the pace that was set, and not give out and forget himself, and have part of his hand chopped off. There were the "hoisters," as they were called, whose task it was to press the lever which lifted the dead cattle off the floor. They ran along upon a rafter, peering down through the damp and the steam; and as old Durham's architect had not built the killing-room for the convenience of the hoisters, at every few feet they would have to stoop under a beam, say four feet above the one they ran on; which got them in the habit of stooping, so that in a few years they would be walking like chimpanzees. Worst of any, however, were the fertilizer-men, and those who served in the cooking-rooms. These people could not be shown to the visitor at a hundred yards, and as for the other men, who worked in the tank-rooms full of steam, and in some of which there were open vats near the level of the floor, their particular trouble was that they fell into the vats and when they were fished out, there was never enough to be worth exhibiting,—sometimes they would be overlooked for days, till all but the bones of them had gone out to the world as Durham's Pure Leaf Lard!

QUESTIONS TO CONSIDER

1. What public health issues does Sinclair expose?

2. What issues for immigrant workers does Sinclair reveal?

3. Why do you think that *The Jungle* brought about reform for food purity but not for immigrant workers?

Choosing a Dream

BY MARIO PUZO

In this excerpt from The Immigrant Experience: The Anguish of Becoming American, *famous novelist Mario Puzo (author of* The Godfather*) reflects on his childhood in Manhattan's Hell's Kitchen neighborhood during the 1920s and '30s. Like many second-generation immigrant children, he had strong ties to the old customs but also was drawn to the new American culture. His account does not ignore the difficulties, but he finds in his childhood the roots of his later success and happiness.*

As a child and in my adolescence, living in the heart of New York's Neapolitan[1] ghetto, I never heard an Italian singing. None of the grown-ups I knew were charming or loving or understanding. Rather they seemed coarse, vulgar, and insulting. And so later in my life when I was exposed to all the clichés of lovable Italians, singing Italians, happy-go-lucky Italians, I wondered where . . . the moviemakers and storywriters got all their ideas from.

---

[1] Neapolitan—Italian from Naples.

At a very early age I decided to escape these **uncongenial**[2] folk by becoming an artist, a writer. It seemed then an impossible dream. My father and mother were illiterate, as were their parents before them. But practicing my art I tried to view the adults with a more charitable eye and so came to the conclusion that their only fault lay in their being foreigners; I was an American. This didn't really help because I was only half right. I was the foreigner. They were already more "American" than I could ever become.

But it did seem then that the Italian immigrants, all the fathers and mothers that I knew, were a grim lot; always shouting, always angry, quicker to quarrel than embrace. I did not understand that their lives were a long labor to earn their daily bread and that physical fatigue does not sweeten human natures.

And so even as a very small child I dreaded growing up to be like the adults around me. I heard them saying too many cruel things about their dearest friends, saw too many of their false embraces with those they had just **maligned**,[3] observed with horror their paranoiac[4] anger at some small slight or a fancied injury to their pride. They were, always, too unforgiving. In short, they did not have the careless **magnanimity**[5] of children.

In my youth I was contemptuous of my elders, including a few under thirty. I thought my contempt special to their circumstances. Later when I wrote about these illiterate men and women, when I thought I understood them, I felt a condescending pity. After all, they had suffered, they had labored all the days of their lives. They had never tasted luxury, knew little more economic security than those ancient Roman slaves who might

---

[2] **uncongenial**—unpleasant.

[3] **maligned**—criticized.

[4] paranoiac—irrationally suspicious.

[5] **magnanimity**—generosity.

have been their ancestors. And alas, I thought, with new-found artistic insight, they were cut off from their children because of the strange American tongue, alien to them, native to their sons and daughters.

Already an artist but not yet a husband or father, I pondered **omnisciently**[6] on their tragedy, again thinking it special circumstance rather than a constant in the human condition. I did not yet understand why these men and women were willing to settle for less than they deserved in life and think that "less" quite a bargain. I did not understand that they simply could not afford to dream, I myself had a hundred dreams from which to choose. For I was already sure that I would make my escape, that I was one of the chosen. I would be rich, famous, happy. I would master my destiny.

And so it was perhaps natural that as a child, with my father gone, my mother the family chief, I, like all the children in all the ghettos of America, became locked in a bitter struggle with the adults responsible for me. It was inevitable that my mother and I became enemies.

As a child I had the usual dreams. I wanted to be handsome, specifically as cowboy stars in movies were handsome. I wanted to be a killer hero in a world-wide war. Or if no wars came along (our teachers told us another was impossible), I wanted at the very least to be a footloose adventurer. Then I branched out and thought of being a great artist, and then, getting ever more sophisticated, a great criminal.

My mother, however, wanted me to be a railroad clerk. And that was her *highest* ambition; she would have settled for less. At the age of sixteen when I let every-body know that I was going to be a great writer, my friends and family took the news quite calmly, my mother included. She did not become angry. She quite simply assumed that I had gone off my nut. She was illiterate

---

[6] **omnisciently**—all-knowingly.

and her peasant life in Italy made her believe that only a son of the nobility could possibly be a writer. Artistic beauty after all could spring only from the seedbed of fine clothes, fine food, luxurious living. So then how was it possible for a son of hers to be an artist? She was not too convinced she was wrong even after my first two books were published many years later. It was only after the commercial success of my third novel that she gave me the title of poet.

My family and I grew up together on Tenth Avenue, between Thirtieth and Thirty-first streets, part of the area called Hell's Kitchen. This particular neighborhood could have been a movie set for one of the Dead End Kid flicks or for the social drama of the East Side in which John Garfield played the hero. Our tenements were the western wall of the city. Beneath our windows were the vast black iron gardens of the New York Central Railroad, absolutely blooming with stinking boxcars freshly unloaded of cattle and pigs for the city slaughterhouse. Steers sometimes escaped and **loped**[7] through the heart of the neighborhood followed by astonished young boys who had never seen a live cow.

The railroad yards stretched down to the Hudson River, beyond whose garbagey waters rose the rocky Palisades of New Jersey. There were railroad tracks running downtown on Tenth Avenue itself to another freight station called St. Johns Park. Because of this, because these trains cut off one side of the street from the other, there was a wooden bridge over Tenth Avenue, a romantic-looking bridge despite the fact that no sparkling water, no silver flying fish darted beneath it; only heavy dray carts drawn by tired horses, some flat-boarded trucks, tin lizzie automobiles and, of course, long strings of freight cars drawn by black, ugly engines.

---

[7] **loped**—galloped easily.

What was really great, truly magical, was sitting on the bridge, feet dangling down, and letting the engine under you blow up clouds of steam that made you disappear, then reappear all damp and smelling of fresh ironing. When I was seven years old I fell in love for the first time with the tough little girl who held my hand and disappeared with me in that magical cloud of steam. This experience was probably more traumatic and damaging to my later relationships with women than one of those ugly childhood adventures Freudian novelists use to explain why their hero has gone bad.

My father supported his wife and seven children by working as a track man laborer for the New York Central Railroad. My oldest brother worked for the railroad as a brakeman, another brother was a railroad shipping clerk in the freight office. Eventually I spent some of the worst months of my life as the railroad's worst messenger boy.

My oldest sister was just as unhappy as a dressmaker in the garment industry. She wanted to be a school teacher. At one time or another my other two brothers also worked for the railroad—it got all six males in the family. The two girls and my mother escaped, though my mother felt it her duty to send all our bosses a gallon of homemade wine on Christmas. But everybody hated their jobs except my oldest brother who had a night shift and spent most of his working hours sleeping in freight cars. My father finally got fired because the foreman told him to get a bucket of water for the crew and not to take all day. My father took the bucket and disappeared forever.

Nearly all the Italian men living on Tenth Avenue supported their large families by working on the railroad. Their children also earned pocket money by stealing ice from the refrigerator cars in summer and coal from the open stoking cars in the winter. Sometimes an older lad would break the seal of a freight car and take a look inside. But this usually brought down the "Bulls," the special railroad police. And usually the freight was "heavy" stuff, too much work to cart away and sell, something like fresh produce or boxes of cheap candy that nobody would buy.

The older boys, the ones just approaching voting age, made their easy money by hijacking silk trucks that loaded up at the garment factory on Thirty-first Street. They would then sell the expensive dresses door to door, at bargain prices no discount house could match. From this some graduated into organized crime, whose talent scouts alertly tapped young boys versed in strong-arm. Yet despite all this, most of the kids grew up honest, content with fifty bucks a week as truck drivers, deliverymen, and white-collar clerks in the civil service.

I had every desire to go wrong but I never had a chance. The Italian family structure was too **formidable**.[8]

I never came home to an empty house; there was always the smell of supper cooking. My mother was always there to greet me, sometimes with a policeman's club in her hand (nobody ever knew how she acquired it). But she was always there, or her authorized deputy, my older sister, who preferred throwing empty milk bottles at the heads of her little brothers when they got bad marks on their report cards. During the great Depression of the 1930s, though we were the poorest of the poor, I never remember not dining well. Many years later as a guest of a millionaire's club, I realized that our poor family on home relief ate better than some of the richest people in America.

My mother would never dream of using anything but the finest imported olive oil, the best Italian cheeses. My father had access to the fruits coming off ships, the produce from railroad cars, all before it went through the stale process of middlemen; and my mother, like most Italian women, was a fine cook in the peasant style.

---

[8] **formidable**—overpowering.

My mother was as formidable a personage as she was a cook. She was not to be treated **cavalierly**.[9] My oldest brother at age sixteen had his own tin lizzie Ford and used it to further his career as the Don Juan of Tenth Avenue. One day my mother asked him to drive her to the market on Ninth Avenue and Fortieth Street, no more than a five-minute trip. My brother had other plans and claimed he was going to work on a new shift on the railroad. Work was an acceptable excuse even for funerals. But an hour later when my mother came out of the door of the tenement she saw the tin lizzie loaded with three pretty neighborhood girls, my Don Juan brother about to drive them off. Unfortunately there was a cobblestone lying loose in the gutter. My mother dropped her black leather shopping bag and picked up the stone with both hands. As we all watched in horror, she brought the boulder down on the nearest fender of the tin lizzie, demolishing it. Then she picked up her bag and marched off to Ninth Avenue to do her shopping. To this day, forty years later, my brother's voice still has a surprised horror and shock when he tells the story. He still doesn't understand how she could have done it.

My mother had her own legends and myths on how to amass a fortune. There was one of our uncles who worked as an assistant chef in a famous Italian-style restaurant. Every day, six days a week, this uncle brought home, under his shirt, six eggs, a stick of butter, and a small bag of flour. By doing this for thirty years he was able to save enough money to buy a $15,000 house on Long Island and two smaller houses for his son and daughter. Another cousin, blessed with a college degree, worked as a chemist in a large manufacturing firm. By using the firm's raw materials and equipment he concocted a superior floor wax which he sold door to door in his spare time. It was a great floor wax and with his

---

[9] **cavalierly**—offhandedly, with arrogant disregard.

low overhead, the price was right. My mother and her friend did not think this stealing. They thought of it as being thrifty. . . .

As rich men escape their wives by going to their club, I finally escaped my mother by going to the Hudson Guild Settlement House. Most people do not know that a settlement house is really a club combined with social services. The Hudson Guild, a five-story field of joy for slum kids, had ping pong rooms and billiard rooms, a shop in which to make lamps, a theater for putting on amateur plays, a gym to box and play basketball in. And then there were individual rooms where your particular club could meet in privacy. The Hudson Guild even suspended your membership for improper behavior or failure to pay the tiny dues. It was a **heady**[10] experience for a slum kid to see his name posted on the billboard to the effect that he was suspended by the Board of Governors.

There were young men who guided us as counselors whom I remember with fondness to this day. They were more like friends than adults assigned to watch over us. I still remember one helping us eat a box of stolen chocolates rather than reproaching us. Which was exactly the right thing for him to do; we trusted him after that. The Hudson Guild kept more kids out of jail than a thousand policemen. It still exists today, functioning for the new immigrants, the blacks, and the Puerto Ricans.

There was a night when the rich people of New York, including the Ethical Culture Society, attended a social function at the Hudson Guild in order to be conned into contributing huge sums of money for the settlement house program. I think it was a dinner and amateur theater presentation that was costing them a hundred bucks a head. Their chauffeurs parked the limousines all along the curbs of Twenty-seventh Street and

---

[10] **heady**—exciting.

Tenth Avenue. Us deprived kids, myself the leader, spent the night letting the air out of our benefactors' tires. *Noblesse oblige.*[11]

But we weren't all bad. In our public schools one year an appeal was made to every child to try to bring a can of food to fill Thanksgiving baskets for the poor. The teachers didn't seem to realize *we* were the poor. We didn't either. Every kid in that public school, out of the goodness of his heart, went out and stole a can of food from a local grocery store. Our school had the best contributor record of any school in the city.

Some of the most exciting days in my life were spent at the Hudson Guild. At the age of eleven I became captain of my club football team for seven years, and president of the Star Club, an office I held for five. I enjoyed that success more than any other in my life. And learned a great deal from it. At the age of fifteen I was as thoroughly corrupted by power as any dictator until I was overthrown by a coalition of votes; my best friends joining my enemies to depose me. It was a rare lesson to learn at fifteen.

The Star Club was made up of boys my own age, a gang, really, which had been pacified by the Hudson Guild Settlement House. We had a football team, a baseball team, a basketball team. We had a yearbook. We had our own room, where we could meet, and a guidance counselor, usually a college boy. We had one named Ray Dooley whom I remember with affection to this day. He took us for outings in the country, to the Hudson Guild Farm in New Jersey for winter weekends where we hitched our sleds to his car, towed at thirty miles an hour. We repaid him by throwing lye into his face and almost blinding him. We thought it was flour. He never reproached us and it wound up OK. We idolized him

---

[11] *Noblesse oblige*—(French) duty of the rich to aid the poor. Puzo is turning the meaning of the term around.

after that. I liked him because he never tried to **usurp**[12] my power, not so that I could notice.

The Hudson Guild was also responsible for absolutely the happiest times of my childhood. When I was about nine or ten they sent me away as a Fresh Air Fund kid. This was a program where slum children were boarded on private families in places like New Hampshire for two weeks.

As a child I knew only the stone city. I had no conception of what the countryside could be. When I got to New Hampshire, when I smelled grass and flowers and trees, when I ran barefoot along the dirt country roads, when I drove the cows home from pasture, when I darted through fields of corn and waded through clear brooks, when I gathered warm brown speckled eggs in the henhouse, when I drove a hay wagon drawn by two great horses—when I did all these things, I nearly went crazy with the joy of it. It was quite simply a fairy tale come true.

The family that took me in, a middle-aged man and woman, childless, were Baptists and observed Sunday so religiously that even checker playing was not allowed on the Lord's day of rest. We went to church on Sunday for a good three hours, counting Bible class, then again at night. On Thursday evenings we went to prayer meetings. My guardians, out of religious **scruple**,[13] had never seen a movie. They disapproved of dancing, they were no doubt political reactionaries; they were everything that I came later to fight against.

And yet they gave me those magical times children never forget. For two weeks every summer from the time I was nine to fifteen I was happier than I have ever been before or since. The man was good with tools and built me a little playground with swings, sliding ponds, see-saws. The woman had a beautiful flower and vegetable

---

[12] **usurp**—overturn.

[13] **scruple**—principle.

garden and let me pick from it. A cucumber or strawberry in the earth was a miracle. And then when they saw how much I loved picnics, the sizzling frankfurters on a stick over the wood fire, the yellow roasted corn, they drove me out on Sunday afternoons to a lovely green grass mountainside. Only on Sundays it was never called a picnic, it was called "taking our lunch outside." I found it—then and now—a sweet **hypocrisy**.[14]

The Baptist preacher lived in the house a hundred yards away and so sometimes he, too, took his lunch "out" with us on a Sunday afternoon, he and his wife and children. Outside of his church he was a jolly fat man, a repressed comedian. Also a fond father, he bought his children a great many toys. I borrowed those toys and on one late August day I sailed his son's huge motor launch down a quiet, winding brook and when it nosed into a wet mossy bank I buried the toy there to have the following year when I came back. But I never found it.

There came a time, I was fifteen, when I was told I was too old to be sent away to the country as a Fresh Air Fund kid. It was the first real warning that I must enter the adult world, ready or not. But I always remembered that man and woman with affection, perhaps more. They always bought me clothing during my visits, my very first pajamas. They sent me presents at Christmastime, and when I was about to go into the army I visited them as a young man of twenty-one. . . .

I believed then, as a child, that the State of New Hampshire had some sort of gates at which all thieves and bad guys were screened out. I believed this, I think, because the house was left unlocked when we went to church on Sundays and Thursday nights. I believed it because I never heard anyone curse or quarrel with raised voices. I believed it because it was beautiful to believe.

---

[14] **hypocrisy**—pretense.

When I returned home from these summer vacations I had a new trick. I said grace with bowed head before eating the familiar spaghetti and meat balls. My mother always tolerated this for the few days it lasted. After all, the two weeks' vacation from her most troublesome child was well worth a Baptist prayer.

From this Paradise I was flung into Hell. That is, I had to help support my family by working on the railroad. After school hours of course. This was the same railroad that had supplied free coal and free ice to the whole Tenth Avenue when I was young enough to steal with impunity. After school finished at 3 p.m. I went to work in the freight office as a messenger. I also worked Saturdays and Sundays when there was work available.

I hated it. One of my first short stories was about how I hated that job. But of course what I really hated was entering the adult world. To me the adult world was a dark enchantment, unnatural. As unnatural to the human dream as death. And as inevitable.

The young are impatient about change because they cannot grasp the power of time itself; not only as the enemy of flesh, the very germ of death, but time as a **benign**[15] cancer. As the young cannot grasp really that love must be a victim of time, so too they cannot grasp that injustices, the economic and family traps of living, can also fall victim to time.

And so I really thought that I would spend the rest of my life as a railroad clerk. That I would never be a writer. That I would be married and have children and go to christenings and funerals and visit my mother on a Sunday afternoon. That I would never own an automobile or a house. That I would never see Europe, the Paris and Rome and Greece I was reading about in books from the public library. That I was hopelessly trapped by my family, by society, by my lack of skills and education.

---

[15] **benign**—of no danger to health; not malignant.

But I escaped again. At the age of eighteen I started dreaming about the happiness of my childhood. As later at the age of thirty I would dream about the joys of my lost adolescence, as at the age of thirty-five I was to dream about the wonderful time I had in the army which I had hated being in. As at the age of forty-five I dreamed about the happy, struggling years of being a devoted husband and loving father. I had the most valuable of human gifts, that of retrospective falsification: remembering the good and not the bad.

I still dreamed of future glory. I still wrote short stories, one or two a year. I still *KNEW* I would be a great writer but I was beginning to realize that accidents could happen and my second choice, that of being a great criminal, was coming up fast. But for the young everything goes so slowly, I could wait it out. The world would wait for me. I could still spin out my life with dreams.

In the summertime I was one of the great Tenth Avenue athletes but in the wintertime I became a sissy. I read books. At a very early age I discovered libraries, the one in the Hudson Guild and the public ones. I loved reading in the Hudson Guild where the librarian became a friend. I loved Joseph Altsheler's (I don't even have to look up his name) tales about the wars of the New York State Indian tribes, the Senecas and the Iroquois. I discovered Doc Savage and the Shadow and then the great Sabatini.[16] Part of my character to this day is Scaramouche,[17] I like to think. And then maybe at the age of fourteen or fifteen or sixteen I discovered Dostoyevsky.[18] I read the books, all of them I could get. I

---

[16] Sabatini—Rafael Sabatini, Italian-born English writer (1875–1950).

[17] Scaramouche—title character of Sabatini's novel, who seeks to avenge a friend's death at the hands of an evil aristocrat.

[18] Dostoyevsky—Fyodor Mikhailovich Dostoyevsky (1821–1881), a famous Russian novelist.

wept for Prince Myshkin in *The Idiot*, I was as guilty as Raskolnikov. And when I finished *The Brothers Karamazov* I understood for the first time what was really happening to me and the people around me. I had always hated religion even as a child but now I became a true believer. I believed in art. A belief that has helped me as well as any other.

My mother looked on all this reading with a fishy Latin eye. She saw no profit in it but since all her children were great readers she was a good enough general to know she could not fight so pervasive an **insubordination**.[19] And there may have been some envy. If she had been able to she would have been the greatest reader of us all.

My direct ancestors for a thousand years have most probably been illiterate. Italy, the golden land, so loving to vacationing Englishmen, so majestic in its language and cultural treasures (they call it, I think, the cradle of civilization), has never cared for its poor people. My father and mother were both illiterates. Both grew up on rocky, hilly farms in the countryside adjoining Naples. My mother remembers never being able to taste the ham from the pig they slaughtered every year. It brought too high a price in the marketplace and cash was needed. My mother was also told the family could not afford the traditional family gift of linens when she married and it was this that decided her to emigrate to America to marry her first husband, a man she barely knew. When he died in a tragic work accident on the docks, she married my father, who assumed responsibility for a widow and her four children perhaps out of ignorance, perhaps out of compassion, perhaps out of love. Nobody ever knew. He was a mystery, a Southern Italian with blue eyes who departed from the family scene three children later when I was twelve. But he cursed Italy even more than my mother did. Then again, he wasn't too pleased

---

[19] **insubordination**—disobedience.

with America either. My mother never heard of Michelangelo;[20] the great deeds of the Caesars[21] had not yet reached her ears. She never heard the great music of her native land. She could not sign her name.

And so it was hard for my mother to believe that her son could become an artist. After all, her one dream in coming to America had been to earn her daily bread, a wild dream in itself. And looking back she was dead right. Her son an artist? To this day she shakes her head. I shake mine with her.

America may be a **fascistic**,[22] warmongering, racially prejudiced country today. It may deserve the hatred of its revolutionary young. But what a miracle it once was! What has happened here has never happened in any other country in any other time. The poor who had been poor for centuries— . . . since the beginning of Christ—whose children had inherited their poverty, their illiteracy, their hopelessness, achieved some economic dignity and freedom. You didn't get it for nothing, you had to pay a price in tears, in suffering, but why not? And some even became artists.

Not even my gift for retrospective falsification can make my eighteenth to twenty-first years seem like a happy time. I hated my life. I was being dragged into the trap I feared and had foreseen even as a child. It was all there, the steady job, the nice girl . . . and then the marriage and fighting over counting pennies to make ends meet. I noticed myself acting more unheroic all the time. I had to tell lies in pure self-defense, I did not forgive so easily.

But I was delivered. When World War II broke out I was delighted. There is no other word, terrible as it may sound. My country called. I was delivered from my mother, my family, the girl I was loving passionately but did not love. And delivered WITHOUT GUILT. Heroically.

---

[20] Michelangelo—Michelangelo Buonarroti (1475–1564), a famous Italian painter and sculptor.

[21] Caesars—emperors of ancient Rome.

[22] **fascistic**—like the fascist governments of Hitler and Mussolini (in this case warlike, super nationalistic, and racist).

My country called, ordered me to defend it. I must have been one of millions, sons, husbands, fathers, lovers, making their innocent getaway from baffled loved ones. And what an escape it was. The war made all my dreams come true. I drove a jeep, toured Europe, had love affairs, found a wife, and lived the material for my first novel. But of course that was a just war as Vietnam is not, and so today it is perhaps for the best that the revolutionary young make their escape by attacking their own rulers.

Then why five years later did I walk back into the trap with a wife and child and a civil service job I was glad to get? After five years of the life I had dreamed about, plenty of women, plenty of booze, plenty of money, hardly any work, interesting companions, travel, etc., why did I walk back into that cage of family and duty and a steady job?

For the simple reason, of course, that I had never really escaped, not my mother, not my family, not the moral pressures of our society. Time again had done its work. I was back in my cage and I was, I think, happy. In the next twenty years I wrote three novels.[23] Two of them were critical successes but I didn't make much money. The third novel, not as good as the others, made me rich. And free at last. Or so I thought.

Then why do I dream of those immigrant Italian peasants as having been happy? I remember how they spoke of their forebears, who spent all their lives farming the arid mountain slopes of Southern Italy. "He died in that house in which he was born," they say enviously. "He was never more than an hour from his village, not in all his life," they sigh. And what would they make of a phrase like "retrospective falsification"?

No, really, we are all happier now. It is a better life. And after all, as my mother always said, "Never mind about being happy. Be glad you're alive."

When I came to my "autobiographical novel," the one every writer does about himself, I planned to make

---

[23] three novels—*The Dark Arena*, *The Fortunate Pilgrim*, and *The Godfather*.

myself the sensitive, misunderstood hero, much put upon by his mother and family. To my astonishment my mother took over the book and instead of my revenge I got another comeuppance. But it is, I think, my best book. And all those old-style grim conservative Italians whom I hated, then pitied so patronizingly, they also turned out to be heroes. Through no desire of mine. I was surprised. The thing that amazed me most was their courage. Where were their Congressional Medals of Honor? Their Distinguished Service Crosses? How did they ever . . . get married, have kids, go out to earn a living in a strange land, with no skills, not even knowing the language? They made it without tranquillizers, without sleeping pills, without psychiatrists, without even a dream. Heroes. Heroes all around me. I never saw them.

But how could I? They wore lumpy work clothes and handlebar moustaches, they blew their noses on their fingers and they were so short that their high-school children towered over them. They spoke a laughable broken English and the furthest limit of their horizon was their daily bread. Brave men, brave women, they fought to live their lives without dreams. Bent on survival they narrowed their minds to the thinnest line of existence.

It is no wonder that in my youth I found them contemptible. And yet they had left Italy and sailed the ocean to come to a new land and leave their sweated bones in America. Illiterate Colombos,[24] they dared to seek the promised land. And so they, too, dreamed a dream.

Forty years ago, in 1930, when I was ten, I remember gas light, spooky, making the tenement halls and rooms alive with ghosts.

We had the best apartment on Tenth Avenue, a whole top floor of six rooms, with the hall as our storage cellar and the roof as our patio. Two views, one of the railroad yards backed by the Jersey shore, the other of a

---

[24] Puzo is comparing the Italian immigrant men of his childhood to Christopher Columbus, Cristoforo Columbo in Italian.

backyard teeming with tomcats everybody shot at with BB guns. In between these two rooms with a view were three bedrooms without windows—the classic railroad flat pattern. The kitchen had a fire escape that I used to sneak out at night. I liked that apartment though it had no central heating, only a coal stove at one end and an oil stove at the other. I remember it as comfortable, slum or not.

My older brothers listened to a crystal radio on homemade headsets. I hitched a ride on the backs of horses and wagons, my elders daringly rode the trolley cars. Only forty years ago in calendar time, it is really a thousand years in terms of change in our physical world.

QUESTIONS TO CONSIDER

1. Why does Puzo say, "It was inevitable that my mother and I became enemies"? How did she influence his life?

2. How did the Italian family structure keep most children from "going wrong"?

3. What influence did the Hudson Guild have on "slum kids," including the author?

4. What factors help to explain how Puzo escaped the confines of the ghetto?

Old Country Advice

BY WILLIAM SAROYAN

William Saroyan (1905–1981) was the son of an Armenian immigrant who died when Saroyan was only six. On seeing some of his father's writing at the age of nine, he was inspired to become a writer. Like many other acclaimed American authors, Saroyan writes about the process by which immigrant families became American. He records how the older generations often relate to the new country from their foreign perspective. Younger family members are required to respect their elders, yet they adjust more quickly to American culture. The following story is from a collection called My Name Is Aram, *published in 1939. Here, Saroyan sees the humorous side of generational differences in a story about Aram's uncle and the advice his uncle gave him before he took a long trip. The first part, from the Preface, is Saroyan's explanation of the book and his not-so-satisfactory answer as to whether it is autobiographical.*

From the Preface

As far as I am able to tell, what this book is is the story of an American boy named Aram Garoghlanian. I do not pretend that the story has any plot, and I hereby give fair warning that nothing extraordinary is going to happen in it.

The way to pronounce that name is to say *Gar*, pause, *oghlan*, slight pause, *ian*. The name is an Armenian name made of two Turkish words, *gar*, meaning dark or possibly black, and *oghlan*, meaning, unmistakably and without qualification, son; *ian*, meaning, naturally, of that tribe. In short, Garoghlanian Aram, meaning Aram of the dark or black sons. Which may not be a matter of the very greatest importance to anybody this year, but may take on an appropriately modest importance later on. As to whether or not the writer himself is Aram Garoghlanian, the writer cannot very well say. He will, however, say that he is not, certainly, *not* Aram Garoghlanian.

Old Country Advice

One year my uncle Melik traveled from Fresno to New York. Before he got aboard the train his uncle Garro paid him a visit and told him about the dangers of travel.

When you get on the train, the old man said, choose your seat carefully, sit down, and do not look about.

Yes, sir, my uncle said.

Several moments after the train begins to move, the old man said, two men wearing uniforms will come down the aisle and ask you for your ticket. Ignore them. They will be **impostors**.[1]

How will I know? my uncle said.

You will know, the old man said. You are no longer a child.

Yes, sir, my uncle said.

Before you have traveled twenty miles an **amiable**[2] young man will come to you and offer you a cigarette. Tell him you don't smoke. The cigarette will be doped.

---

[1] **impostors**—fakes; deceivers who appear to be people they are not.

[2] **amiable**—friendly.

Yes, sir, said my uncle.

On your way to the diner a very beautiful young woman will bump into you intentionally and almost embrace you, the old man said. She will be extremely apologetic and attractive, and your natural impulse will be to cultivate her friendship. Dismiss your natural impulse and go on in and eat. The woman will be an adventuress.

A what? my uncle said.

A whore, the old man shouted. Go on in and eat. Order the best food, and if the diner is crowded, and the beautiful young woman sits across the table from you, do not look into her eyes. If she speaks, pretend to be deaf.

Yes, sir, my uncle said.

Pretend to be deaf, the old man said. That is the only way out of it.

Out of what? my uncle said.

Out of the whole ungodly mess, the old man said. I have traveled. I know what I'm talking about.

Yes, sir, my uncle said.

Let's say no more about it, the old man said.

Yes, sir, my uncle said.

Let's not speak of the matter again, the old man said. It's finished. I have seven children. My life has been a full and righteous one. Let's not give it another thought. I have land, vines, trees, cattle, and money. One cannot have everything—except for a day or two at a time.

Yes, sir, my uncle said.

On your way back to your seat from the diner, the old man said, you will pass through the smoker.[3] There you will find a game of cards in progress. The players will be three middle-aged men with expensive-looking rings on their fingers. They will nod at you pleasantly and one of them will invite you to join the game. Tell them, No speak English.

---

[3] smoker—railroad parlor car set aside for those who wished to smoke.

Yes, sir, my uncle said.

That is all, the old man said.

Thank you very much, my uncle said.

One thing more, the old man said. When you go to bed at night, take your money out of your pocket and put it in your shoe. Put your shoe under your pillow, keep your head on the pillow all night, *and don't sleep.*

Yes, sir, my uncle said.

That is all, the old man said.

The old man went away and the next day my uncle Melik got aboard the train and traveled straight across America to New York. The two men in uniforms were not impostors, the young man with the doped cigarette did not arrive, the beautiful young woman did not sit across the table from my uncle in the diner, and there was no card game in progress in the smoker. My uncle put his money in his shoe and put his shoe under his pillow and put his head on the pillow and didn't sleep all night the first night, but the second night he abandoned the whole ritual.

The second day he *himself* offered another young man a cigarette which the other young man accepted. In the diner my uncle went out of his way to sit at a table with a young lady. He started a poker game in the smoker, and long before the train ever got to New York my uncle knew everybody aboard the train and everybody knew him. Once, while the train was traveling through Ohio, my uncle and the young man who had accepted the cigarette and two young ladies on their way to Vassar formed a quartette and sang "The Wabash Blues."

The journey was a very pleasant one.

When my uncle Melik came back from New York, his old uncle Garro visited him again.

I see you are looking all right, he said. Did you follow my instructions?

Yes, sir, my uncle said.

The old man looked far away in space.

I am pleased that *someone* has profited by my experience, he said.

QUESTIONS TO CONSIDER

1. What views of American life did Garro's advice to Melik reveal?

2. Why didn't Melik follow his uncle's advice?

3. How do you think the author feels about his immigrant relatives? Explain.

from

The Education of Hyman Kaplan

BY LEO ROSTEN

After the surge of non-English-speaking immigrants flooded the country in the early twentieth century, night schools for adults appeared in many major American cities. By the 1930s, thousands of adult immigrants attended classes whose main purpose was to prepare them to become naturalized citizens. In these schools, they were taught the English language, American customs, and American history. Humorist Leo Rosten describes a dedicated teacher's efforts to Americanize his most challenging student at the American Night Preparatory School for Adults and the unexpected, amusing results.

In the third week of the new term, Mr. Parkhill was forced to the conclusion that Mr. Kaplan's case was rather difficult. Mr. Kaplan first came to his special attention, out of the thirty-odd adults in the beginners' grade of the American Night Preparatory School for Adults

("English—Americanization—Civics—Preparation for Naturalization"), through an exercise the class had submitted. The exercise was entitled "Fifteen Common Nouns and Their Plural Forms." Mr. Parkhill came to one paper which included the following:

```
house . . . . makes . . . . houses
dog  . . . . . . . "  . . . . . . dogies
libary . . . . . . "  . . . . . . Public libary
cat  . . . . . . . . "  . . . . . . Katz
```

Mr. Parkhill read this over several times, very thoughtfully. He decided that here was a student who might, unchecked, develop into a "problem case." It was clearly a case that called for special attention. He turned the page over and read the name. It was printed in large, firm letters with red crayon. Each letter was outlined in blue. Between every two letters was a star, carefully drawn, in green. The multi-colored whole spelled, unmistakably, H*Y*M*A*N K*A*P*L*A*N.

This Mr. Kaplan was in his forties, a plump, red-faced gentleman, with wavy blond hair, *two* fountain pens in his outer pocket, and a perpetual smile. It was a strange smile, Mr. Parkhill remarked: vague, bland, and consistent in its **monotony**.[1] The thing that emphasized it for Mr. Parkhill was that it never seemed to leave the face of Mr. Kaplan, even during Recitation and Speech period. This disturbed Mr. Parkhill considerably, because Mr. Kaplan was particularly bad in Recitation and Speech.

Mr. Parkhill decided he had not applied himself as conscientiously as he might to Mr. Kaplan's case. That very night he called on Mr. Kaplan first.

"Won't *you* take advantage of Recitation and Speech practice, Mr. Kaplan?" he asked, with an encouraging smile.

---

[1] **monotony**—tiresome sameness; lack of variety.

Mr. Kaplan smiled back and answered promptly, "Vell, I'll tell abot Prazidents United States. Fife Prazidents United States is Abram Lincohen; Hodding, Coolitch, Judge Vashington, an' Banjamin Frenklin."

Further encouragement revealed that in Mr. Kaplan's literary Valhalla[2] the "most famous tree American wriders" were Jeck Laundon, Valt Viterman, and the author of "Hawk L. Barry-Feen," one Mocktvain.[3] Mr. Kaplan took pains to point out that he did not mention Relfvaldo Amerson[4] because "He is a poyet, an' I'm talkink abot wriders."

Mr. Parkhill diagnosed the case as one of "inability to distinguish between "a" and "e." He concluded that Mr. Kaplan *would* need special attention. He was, frankly, a little disturbed.

Mr. Kaplan's English showed no improvement during the next hard weeks. The originality of his spelling and pronunciation, however, flourished—like a sturdy flower in the good, rich earth. A man to whom "Katz" is the plural of "cat" soon soars into higher and more ambitious endeavor. As a one-paragraph "Exercise in Composition," Mr. Kaplan submitted:

When people is meating on the boulvard, on going away one is saying, "I am glad I mat you," and the other is giving answer, "Mutual."

Mr. Parkhill felt that perhaps Mr. Kaplan had over-reached himself, and should be confined to the simpler exercises.

Mr. Kaplan was an earnest student. He worked hard, knit his brows regularly (albeit with that smile), did all his homework, and never missed a class. Only once did Mr. Parkhill feel that Mr. Kaplan might, perhaps, be a little

---

[2] Valhalla—the final resting place for the souls of heroes in Norse mythology. A literary Valhalla would include the greatest dead writers.

[3] Hyman Kaplan is referring to Jack London, Walt Whitman, and the author of *Huckleberry Finn*, Mark Twain.

[4] Relfvaldo Amerson—Ralph Waldo Emerson.

more *serious* about his work. That was when he asked Mr. Kaplan to "give a noun."

"Door," said Mr. Kaplan, smiling.

It seemed to Mr. Parkhill that "door" had been given only a moment earlier, by Miss Mitnick.

"Y-es," said Mr. Parkhill. "Er—and another noun?"

"Another door," Mr. Kaplan replied promptly.

Mr. Parkhill put him down as a doubtful "C." Everything pointed to the fact that Mr. Kaplan might have to be kept on an extra three months before he was ready for promotion to Composition, Grammar, and Civics, with Miss Higby.

One night Mrs. Moskowitz read a sentence, from "English for Beginners," in which "the vast deserts of America" were referred to. Mr. Parkhill soon discovered that poor Mrs. Moskowitz did not know the meaning of "vast." "Who can tell us the meaning of 'vast'?" asked Mr. Parkhill lightly.

Mr. Kaplan's hand shot up, volunteering wisdom. He was all proud grins. Mr. Parkhill, in the rashness of the moment, nodded to him.

Mr. Kaplan rose, radiant with joy. "'Vast!' It's com-mink fromm *diraction*. Ve have four diractions: de naut, de sot, de heast, and de vast."

Mr. Parkhill shook his head. "Er—that is 'west,' Mr. Kaplan." He wrote "VAST" and "WEST" on the blackboard. To the class he added, tolerantly, that Mr. Kaplan was apparently thinking of "west," whereas it was "vast" which was under discussion.

This seemed to bring a great light into Mr. Kaplan's inner world. "So is 'vast' vat you eskink?"

Mr. Parkhill admitted that it was "vast" for which he was asking.

"Aha!" cried Mr. Kaplan. "You minn *'vast,'* not"—with scorn—"'vast.'"

"Yes," said Mr. Parkhill, faintly.

"Hau Kay!" said Mr. Kaplan, essaying the vernacular,[5] "Ven I'm buyink a suit clothes, I'm gattink de cawt, de pents, an' de vast!"

Stunned, Mr. Parkhill shook his head, very sadly.

"I'm afraid that you've used still another word, Mr. Kaplan."

Oddly enough, this seemed to give Mr. Kaplan great pleasure.

Several nights later Mr. Kaplan took advantage of Open Questions period. This ten-minute period was Mr. Parkhill's special innovation in the American Night Preparatory School for Adults. It was devoted to answering any questions which the students might care to raise about any difficulties which they might have encountered during the course of their adventures with the language. Mr. Parkhill enjoyed Open Questions. He liked to clear up *practical* problems. He felt he was being ever so much more constructive that way. Miss Higby had once told him that he was a born Open Questions teacher.

"Plizz, Mr. Pockheel," asked Mr. Kaplan as soon as the Period opened. "Vat's de minnink fromm—" It sounded, in Mr. Kaplan's **rendition**,[6] like "a big department."

"'A big department,' Mr. Kaplan?" asked Mr. Parkhill, to make sure.

"Yassir!" Mr. Kaplan's smile was beauteous to behold, "In de stritt, ven I'm valkink, I'm hearink like 'I big de pottment.'"

It was definitely a **pedagogical**[7] opportunity.

"Well, class," Mr. Parkhill began. "I'm sure that you have all—"

He told them that they had all probably done some shopping in the large downtown stores. (Mr. Kaplan

---

[5] essaying the vernacular—trying ordinary, everyday speech.

[6] **rendition**—interpretation; performance.

[7] **pedagogical**—teaching.

nodded.) In these large stores, he said, if they wanted to buy a pair of shoes, for example, they went to a special *part* of the store, where only shoes were sold—a *shoe* department. (Mr. Kaplan nodded.) If they wanted a table, they went to a different *part* of the store, where *tables* were sold. (Mr. Kaplan nodded.) If they wanted to buy, say, a goldfish, they went to still another part of the store, where goldfish . . . (Mr. Kaplan frowned; it was clear that Mr. Kaplan had never bought a goldfish.)

"Well, then," Mr. Parkhill summed up hastily, "each article is sold in a different *place.* These different and special places are called *departments.*"

He printed "D-E-P-A-R-T-M-E-N-T" on the board in large, clear capitals. "And a *big* department, Mr. Kaplan, is merely such a department which is large—*big!*"

He put the chalk down and wiped his fingers.

"Is that clear now, class?" he asked, with a little smile. (It was rather an ingenious explanation, he thought; it might be worth repeating to Miss Higby during the recess.)

It *was* clear. There were thirty nods of approval. But Mr. Kaplan looked uncertain. It was obvious that Mr. Kaplan, a man who would not compromise with truth, did *not* find it clear.

"Isn't that clear *now,* Mr. Kaplan?" asked Mr. Parkhill anxiously.

Mr. Kaplan pursed his lips in thought. "It's a *fine* haxplination, Titcher," he said generously, "but I don' unnistand vy I'm hearink de voids de vay I do. Simms to me it's used in annodder minnink."

"There's really only one meaning for 'a big department.'" Mr. Parkhill was definitely worried by this time. "*If* that's the phrase you mean."

Mr. Kaplan nodded gravely. "Oh, dat's de phrase—ufcawss! It sonds like dat—or maybe a leetle more like '*I* big de pottment.'"

Mr. Parkhill took up the chalk. ("*I* big department" was obviously a case of Mr. Kaplan's own curious audition.[8]) He repeated the explanation carefully, this time embellishing the illustrations with a shirt department, a victrola section, and "a separate part of the store where, for example, you buy canaries, or other birds."

Mr. Kaplan sat entranced. He followed it all politely, even the part about "canaries, or other birds." He smiled throughout with **consummate**[9] reassurance.

Mr. Parkhill was relieved, assuming, in his folly, that Mr. Kaplan's smiles were a testimony to his **exposition**.[10] But when he had finished, Mr. Kaplan shook his head once more, this time with a new and superior firmness.

"Is the explanation *still* not clear?" Mr. Parkhill was genuinely concerned by this time.

"Is de haxplination clear!" cried Mr. Kaplan with enthusiasm. "Ha! I should live so! Soitinly! Clear like *gold*! So clear! An' netcheral too! But Mr. Pockheel—"

"Go on, Mr. Kaplan," said Mr. Parkhill, studying the white dust on his fingers. There was, after all, nothing more to be done.

"Vell! I tink it's more like '*I* big de pottment.'"

"Go on, Mr. Kaplan, go on." (*Domine, dirige nos.*)[11]

Mr. Kaplan rose. His smile was broad, luminous, transcendent; his manner was regal.

"I'm hearink it in de stritt. Sointimes I'm stendink in de stritt, talkink to a frand, or mine vife, mine brodder— or maybe only stendink. An' somvun is pessink arond me. An' by hexident he's givink me a bump, you know, a *poosh*! Vell, he says, 'Axcuse me!' no? But somtimes, an' *dis* is vat I minn, he's sayink, '*I* big de pottment!'"

Mr. Parkhill studied the picture of "Abram Lincohen" on the back wall, as if reluctant to face reality.

---

[8] audition—hearing.

[9] **consummate**—complete; perfect; of the highest degree; excellent.

[10] **exposition**—detailed explanation.

[11] *Domine dirige nos*—(Latin) Lord, direct us.

He wondered whether he could reconcile it with his conscience if he were to promote Mr. Kaplan to Composition, Grammar, and Civics—at once. Another three months of Recitation and Speech might, after all, be nothing but a waste of Mr. Kaplan's valuable time.

QUESTIONS FOR CONSIDERATION

1. What talents does Mr. Kaplan display despite his difficulties with the language?

2. How would you characterize Mr. Parkhill's opinion of Mr. Kaplan? Use evidence from the story in your answer.

3. How much has Mr. Kaplan learned about American culture? What difficulties does he have?

4. Mr. Parkhill's big dilemma is whether or not to promote Mr. Kaplan. Should he? Why or why not?

California Palms

BY LÊ THI DIEM THÚY

In recent years, the United States has granted asylum, or refuge, to thousands of people fleeing from civil war, life-threatening disruptions, and oppression in their home countries. A dramatic example resulted from the Vietnam War, a civil war in which the United States played an active role from the mid-1960s to the early 1970s. Vietnamese citizens caught in the crossfire of war often had to flee their villages and seek protection wherever they could. As the United States began to withdraw its troops during the last years of the war, Vietnamese who had supported the United States looked for ways out of the country, trying to avoid the revenge of the communist victors. After the war ended, many refugees eventually made their way to the United States. Lê thi diem thúy comments not only on the difficulty of adjusting to her new life in America, but also on coming to terms with her childhood memories of life in Vietnam.

Before my mother arrived in the United States from Vietnam, I perceived myself to be an American. Whatever that is. I'd acquired a taste for dill pickles, macaroni and cheese, was an expert at the Hula-Hoop and roller skating backwards. I thought this entitled me to glide along like I imagined everyone else gliding along—merrily—and with no past to speak of. Not only did my mother prompt me to question my taste in American food by reacquainting me with condensed milk, ginger fried fish, lichee nuts, and noodle soup for breakfast, her presence also pointed to an entire history I thought I'd thrown overboard and left for sunken treasure or so much useless luggage adrift in the watery vaults of the Pacific. I thought I had succeeded in making myself light, releasing my longing for Vietnam in order to secure a place in America. Now here was my mother, newly arrived and already dragging memories right out of the sea, shaking them loose on the shore before holding them up to the light and handing them back to me. While my father had instilled in me the belief that we might never go back to Vietnam, my mother came and insisted that we could never leave it.

When my mother arrived in the States in 1980, she had lost three children, survived two wars, was separated from her mother and father, brothers and sisters, and the land of her birth by an entire ocean. My father and I had escaped Vietnam in 1978. During the two years between our departure from Vietnam and my mother's arrival in the United States with my younger sister in 1980, my father and I had sent my mother portraits of ourselves decked out in our best clothes, standing in front of big cars and fancy houses in the wealthy neighborhood of La Jolla, a **virtual**[1] independent republic of San Diego, California. Through so many smiling images, we led her to believe that the hacienda-style house stretching out behind the two giant California palms was indeed our home in America.

She arrived to find we had no house. What's more, I claimed she wasn't my real mother. I held on to this belief for months. Even coupling it with the suspicion

---

[1] **virtual**—being so in essence or effect, though not in fact or in name.

that this man and woman who assumed the roles of my father and mother were in reality Communist spies, and that the young girl of two or three who was supposedly my sister wasn't really my sister but some child who was cast to be the younger sister just as I had been cast to be the older sister in what appeared to be the portrait of a struggling Vietnamese family newly arrived in America.

Where this elaborate drama came from, I do not know except to say that in my worldly travels as an eight-year-old in what were still the Cold War years, I had picked up the common wisdom that the opposite of an American was a Communist. Also, I had a vivid imagination. I was convinced that entire rooms changed once I'd stepped out of them, like a turning stage that twirled one living room away and brought another living room forward, with the same actors in place but in changed costumes and changed characters, which meant that an entirely different drama was about to unfold.

My mother was not overly concerned with having been cast as an impostor mother. After all, she knew she was my mother. She set about correcting my odd Vietnamese—I'd taken to saying things like, "Can I help you shampoo the dishes?" and acquainting herself with English via songs from television commercials. Her two favorite songs were: "This Bud's for you" and "G.E. We bring good things to life!" Which she pronounced "lie." She often sang these songs—in lieu of the traditional lilting Vietnamese lullaby—to the little girl who, oddly, seemed to like them, especially when my mother thrust a cupped hand in the air, as though toasting the little girl with an invisible twelve-ounce can of Budweiser. . . .

I should have known from the moment my mother arrived in the States that she had the upper hand in determining the direction my family would take. As far as she was concerned, he had failed miserably at keeping things together. Not so much because the hacienda in La Jolla was a fiction but rather because he'd gotten two important details about my identity entirely mixed up.

Back in Vietnam, I'd had an older sister who was called Big Girl, whereas I was called Little Girl. Her given name was Thúy and mine was Trang. We weren't often called by our given names, which is why, supposedly, my father confused her given name with mine. In the States, I assumed the name thúy and celebrated my birthday on January 15. Neither my father nor I was troubled by this until my mother arrived to set us straight. For one thing, she let us know, my name was Trang and my birthday was January 12, not the fifteenth. For a fleeting moment, I entertained the possibility of celebrating my birthday twice in one week, but my mother laughed that one off. Then I thought she'd let me relinquish the name thúy which, pronounced "twee" in English, had caused people to laugh into their hands and make jokes about a certain small cartoon character named Tweety Bird. I didn't necessarily feel that Trang, pronounced like a combination of "train" crashing into "tang," was any better, but it was new and, more important, it was supposed to be my name. To this, my mother said no. My older sister, the original thúy, had escaped Vietnam with my mother and younger sister, but she had drowned at the refugee camp in Malaysia.[2] My mother insisted that I keep the name because, due to my father's propitious mistake, it was a part of my older sister that had made it to America. Like a T-shirt stretched to make a tent, I felt my mother's deft logic expanding the familiar one-syllable note of thúy to make room for my dead sister.

The result was, sometimes I felt my name was like an already occupied bed, something I couldn't quite find my place in because someone else was sprawled out and deep in sleep across it. Other times, I felt I had no name

---

[2] Many Vietnamese immigrants first stayed in camps set up by neighboring countries before coming to America.

or hadn't found my real name yet and was using thúy until then. For a while, I even went by the name of Tina because a friend of mine, an African American girl named Lakeisha, thought thúy was a weird and difficult name to remember. I came to think of names in general and of my name in particular as rough skin, loose approximations of the person underneath.

A name, like any word, can be misspelled, mispronounced, kicked around, and then caressed back to life. Sometimes my mother would say my name in such a way that it didn't seem to be spoken so much as sung and, in its singing, made to linger in the air like a musical note. Through such moments, I came to understand that language is alive as sound, as utterance and invocation. I knew that in one breath she was calling to me and to my older sister, to the past in the present, reaching across the ocean's vastness to touch a particular stretch of beach in front of my grandfather's house.

I remembered the house. The neighbor with the pigeon nest on her roof. A particular rainy Tet[3] evening when I wondered if the firecrackers would light. I remembered a younger brother whom my mother had described as no bigger than a marble when he was first born and an older brother who drowned when I was still in Vietnam but whose death I refused to believe in because my mother had told me, "He fell into a hole in the sea," and I thought that just meant he was hiding under water. I remembered the night my father sat me down in my great-uncle's fishing boat and told me to wait there until he returned. It was the night my mother got into a fight with her father and missed the boat that was taking my father and me away from Vietnam.

My childhood belief that entire rooms disappeared behind me hadn't come out of thin air but out of my own experience of leaving Vietnam. After the days and nights at sea, the months at the refugee camp in Singapore, the

---

[3] Tet—the lunar New Year as celebrated in Vietnam.

year and then two with no signs of my mother or other members of my family showing up, as I had imagined they would, my life in Vietnam took on the **aura**[4] of something remote, like a house I had walked so far away from that when I turned back to look at it, I could barely make out the house, let alone the toys I'd left in the courtyard or the people sleeping inside. Vietnam became a kind of darkness, a deep silence that would occasionally be interrupted by sudden memories of a rooster crowing or a pigeon cooing. I would see flashes of someone's face, sometimes my older brother's as he turned to see how close I had come to catching him during a game of chase on the beach. Such memories of Vietnam appeared like intense points of light occasionally capable of piercing through the dark canopy that had come to define my relationship to the past. By the time my mother and sister arrived, I had buried so much of my longing for Vietnam that I could almost believe I had entered the world as a fully formed eight-year-old, emerging from an untraceable black hole.

My mother was the one who alerted me to the **simultaneity**[5] of worlds. She spoke about Vietnam as if it were right around the corner, as alive as where we were, if not more so. While school and mainstream American movies defined Vietnam as a war, from my mother I might have thought there had never been a war, that history hadn't twisted itself around us like a tornado, lifting us up into the heart of it, stomping out our past with a flick of its tail and then depositing us as far from home as possible. She treated the United States like some place we were passing through, made bearable by the belief that no matter how long or how difficult this journey would be, in the end we were still Vietnamese and we would eventually make it back to

---

[4] **aura**—distinctive character or atmosphere rising from and surrounding a person or a thing.

[5] **simultaneity**—quality of existing or occurring at the same time.

Vietnam. According to my mother, every ordeal was a test of our strength, meant to build character. Strange, inexplicable things happened. One night, we had boarded a boat in southern Vietnam. One day, we had landed by plane in Southern California. That was fate.

It was fate that had changed my position in the family from the fourth child to the eldest, and it was fate which demanded that—even though I was a child—I became the representative head of my family. My mother's conversational English at the time consisted of Yes, No, Maybe, Okay, and Why not?—terms that she used inter-changeably to create a cloud of confusion between herself and the listener. My father, who was less **verbose**,[6] favored nodding solemnly or beginning every explana-tion with, My name is. . . , I entered with, Excuse me, Pardon me, What time is it?, Where is, We're just looking for, and Thank you. Through the clarity of my pronunci-ation and the agility of my translation, I was navigating my family through the perils of daily life, from finding milk at the liquor store to locating the correct room to enter at the social services building or the hospital. My mother was impressed with my English. Whenever I spoke, she would gaze into the face of the listening American and observe how my words were smoothing the furrowed brow, unlocking the tight lips, sometimes even **eliciting**[7] a warm smile. While it might have seemed to my mother that my polite yet directed banter could protect my family from dumbfounded stares and prompt dismissal, I felt that I couldn't truly protect us but was merely delaying our inevitable eviction.

At home, my parents applauded my ability to speak English as well as any American and yet not be an American. In public, I carried myself as the representa-tive of a family most of whose members didn't speak English well but harbored no greater dream than to be

---

[6] **verbose**—talkative.

[7] **eliciting**—drawing forth; bringing out; evoking.

Americans. I both hoped and feared that sooner or later I would be found out. The public would discover that my parents had no desire to become Americans, while my parents would realize that I didn't know how or what it meant to be Vietnamese in America. I could translate sentences from one language to another and back again: tell my mother what my teacher said, ask the sales clerk for what my father wanted. Within our family, I could live life in our small apartment as though it were a distant outpost of Vietnam. Yet every time I turned the television on or stepped out of the house, my parents and Vietnam seemed far away, otherworldly. I had been rowing back and forth, in a relentless manner, between two banks of a wide river. Increasingly, what I wanted was to be a burning boat in the middle of the water, visible to both shores yet indecipherable in my fury.

As early as the age of eight, I had begun to run away. It wasn't long before hunger and darkness brought me back home, but then I would go again, escaping the **claustrophobia**[8] of my house to run barefoot through the streets. I'd wander new neighborhoods, look in on other lives, imagine my family stepping out of a station wagon, strolling across the green lawn to unlock the promise of our very own big house. Or, I imagined bringing strangers home to live with us so that they could share the burden of being a witness to my world. I wanted someone to tell me what they saw in my father's **stoic**[9] silence, my mother's talk about fate, my sister's wide-eyed curiosity, and my own uneasy **donning**[10] of a dead sister's name. Add to this my father's drinking, my mother's gambling, and their spectacular fights, which left my sister and me hiding in the bathroom until our fear died down. On the flip side of all the tumult was the

---

[8] **claustrophobia**—fear of being confined.

[9] **stoic**—indifferent to or unaffected by pain or pleasure; resigned to suffering; disciplined.

[10] **donning**—putting on.

obvious affection, how with my mother's urging my father could be convinced to sing. He would begin slowly, softly, a hint of a song approaching from far away, and then his voice would rise and he'd clap his hands together. We'd join my father, keeping time, following his voice as it searched all the tones, high and low and back again, moving like a solitary figure leading us through areas of darkness and of light.

I think I became a writer in part because I wanted to convey in English the quality of my father's voice as he sang a song in Vietnamese or the peculiar truth of my mother's accented English speaking for General Electric when she declared, "G.E. We bring good things to lie!" Similar to the way my mother has secured my sister's passage to this country by having me bear my sister's name, I have arrived at English through Vietnamese and can't hear one language without feeling the presence of the other. When I sit down to write, there is a part of me that isn't laying words down so much as dragging my grandfather's fishing boats, sand-and-salt-speckled, clear across the Pacific and right onto the page, and then there is the part of me that continues to stare out from those portraits my father and I used to send to my mother, of our fabled hacienda in La Jolla. I see myself, one of two bodies framed within the space between two enormous California palms, smiling a winning smile. The girl I was then asks the woman I am today, What do you see? Daring me to speak.

QUESTIONS TO CONSIDER

1. In what ways did the mix-up over the author's given name affect her developing identity as an American?

2. What does the author mean when she describes her memories of Vietnam as a "kind of darkness"? Why do you suppose she remembers Vietnam the way she does?

3. What do the California palms at La Jolla represent to the author?

4. How does this story compare with those of other immigrants you have read?

Attitudes and Policy

Part four

Two Poems

**BY EMMA LAZARUS AND
THOMAS BAILEY ALDRICH**

*The following poems express two continuing, contradictory attitudes
toward immigration. "The New Colossus" was written by Emma
Lazarus in 1883 to aid the pedestal fund drive for the Statue of
Liberty. The poem has become famous, as it is now inscribed on
the statue's pedestal. It reflects pride in welcoming immigrants and
encouraging them to seek their fortune in the land of opportunity.
This perspective values our "nation of immigrants" as a place
where hard work and ambition are justly rewarded no matter what
the individual's nationality. The second poem, "Unguarded Gates,"
written about twenty years later, expresses a contrasting impulse to
protect the status quo by restricting the flow of immigrants, who
seem to threaten established ways of life. American immigration
policy has reflected both points of view, inevitably contradicting
itself over the years.*

The New Colossus

BY EMMA LAZARUS

Not like the brazen giant of Greek fame,[1]
With conquering limbs astride from land to land;
Her at our sea-washed, sunset gates shall stand
A mighty woman with a torch, whose flame
Is the imprisoned lightning, and her name
Mother of Exiles. From her beacon-hand
Glows world-wide welcome; her mild eyes command
The air-bridged harbor that twin cities[2] frame.

"Keep ancient lands, your storied pomp!" cries she
With silent lips. "Give me your tired, your poor,
Your huddled masses yearning to be free,
The wretched refuse of your teeming shore.
Send these, the homeless, tempest-tost to me,
I lift my lamp beside the golden door."[3]

Unguarded Gates

BY THOMAS BAILEY ALDRICH

Wide open and unguarded stand our gates,
Named of the four winds, North, South, East and West;
Portals that lead to an enchanted land
of cities, forests, fields of living gold,
Vast prairies, lordly summits touched with snow,
Majestic rivers sweeping proudly past
The Arab's date-palm and the Norseman's pine—

---

[1] brazen giant of Greek fame—a reference to the Colossus of Rhodes, a giant statue that stood astride the harbor of the ancient Greek city of Rhodes.

[2] twin cities—New York City and Newark, New Jersey.

[3] These last five lines, beginning with "Give me your tired, your poor," have become very well known and have even been set to music. They are often quoted.

A realm wherein are fruits of every zone,
Airs of all climes, for lo! throughout the year
The red rose blossoms somewhere—a rich land,
A later Eden[4] planted in the wilds,
With not an inch of earth within its bound
But if a slave's foot press it sets him free.
Here, it is written, Toil shall have its wage,
And Honor honor, and the humblest man
Stand level with the highest in the law.
Of such a land have men in dungeons dreamed,
And with the vision brightening in their eyes
Gone smiling to the **fagot**[5] and the sword.

Wide open and unguarded stand our gates,
And through them presses a wild **motley**[6] throng—
Men from the Volga and the Tartar steppes,
Featureless figures of the Hoang-Ho,
Malayan, Scythian, Teuton, Kelt, and Slav,
Flying the Old World's poverty and scorn;
These bringing with them unknown gods and **rites**,[7]
Those, tiger passions, here to stretch their claws.
In street and alley what strange tongues are loud,
Accents of menace alien to our air,
Voices that once the Tower of Babel[8] knew!
O Liberty, white Goddess! Is it well
To leave the gates unguarded? On thy breast
Fold Sorrow's children, soothe the hurts of fate,
Lift the downtrodden, but with hand of steel
Stay those who to thy sacred portals come
To waste the gifts of freedom. Have a care

---

[4] Eden—biblical Garden of Eden; paradise.

[5] **fagot**—torch; burning stick.

[6] **motley**—varied.

[7] **rites**—ceremonies.

[8] Tower of Babel—a biblical reference to a tower built by self-righteous men and destroyed by its confused builders when God caused them to speak many different languages.

Lest from thy brow the clustered stars be torn
And trampled in the dust. For so of old
The thronging Goth and Vandal trampled Rome[9]
And where the temples of the Caesars stood
The lean wolf unmolested made her lair.

---

[9] Goth and Vandal trampled Rome—In the fifth century A.D., barbarian tribes, the Goths and the Vandals, overran the capital of the great Roman Empire and destroyed almost every trace of civilization.

QUESTIONS TO CONSIDER

1. What does the Statue of Liberty's lamp symbolize? Why does Lazarus refer to the statue as the "Mother of Exiles"?

2. According to Aldrich, what makes our country an "enchanted land"?

3. What does Aldrich mean by his statement, "wide open and unguarded stand our gates"? What should we do to protect our country?

4. Why do you think that the contrasting attitudes expressed in the two poems have endured throughout most of American history? How could they ever be reconciled?

Statue of Liberty

The Statue of Liberty was a gift from France to the United States, and was designed by French sculptor Frederic Auguste Bartholdi. Originally commissioned as a monument to America's freed slaves, it was unveiled in New York City's harbor in 1886 and became a beacon of hope for immigrants arriving in America from Europe. On the West Coast, the same role was filled by San Francisco's Golden Gate.

▲
Detail Head and Tablet.

▲
Liberty Enlightening the World Unveiling in 1886.

Immigration Laws

*Until relatively recently, immigration legislation in the United States
followed a clearly defined path. First, for many years virtually no
legislation was passed, largely because the nation was growing and
there was plenty of space to expand. Then, starting in the middle
of the nineteenth century, Congress began placing restrictions on
immigration. At first, regulations were minor, but as the twentieth
century approached, large numbers of immigrants were prohibited
from entering the country. Asian immigrants were targeted first,
partly because they competed with natives for jobs on the West
Coast. By the 1920s, many other nationalities were regulated under
some of the most restrictive immigration laws in United States
history. These laws were not abolished until the 1960s.*

The Laws from 1790–1900

1790—**Naturalization Act of 1790** granted citizenship rights to all "free white persons." Even though
immigration was not specifically restricted, citizenship
was extended only to those who fit the category.

1850—**Foreign Miners' Tax** was imposed against the
Chinese. The tax was $3 dollars a month. It attempted to
limit the number of Chinese in California.

1854—California Supreme Court ruled, in *People* v. *Hall*, that the testimony of Chinese, blacks, "**mulattos**"[1] and Native Americans against whites was invalid; finally repealed almost 20 years later in 1872.

1859—Chinese were excluded from San Francisco public schools.

1864—The first U.S. immigration law was created. It encouraged immigration, but barred criminals and prostitutes from entering the country.

1880—California Civil Code was amended to prohibit inter-racial marriages between a white person and a "Negro, Mulatto, or Mongolian"; Filipinos were later added to this list in 1933. The law was finally repealed in 1948.

1882—**Chinese Exclusion Act of 1882** was the first immigration law to exclude virtually all immigrants from a single country. This act banned Chinese laborers from emigrating to the United States for ten years and prohibited them from becoming citizens. It also banned convicts and the insane.

1898—After the end of the Spanish-American War, the Philippines were given to the United States. Filipinos were declared "wards" and needed no visas to travel to the United States.

The Laws from 1900–1940

1902—Congress extended the prohibition against Chinese immigration, first imposed by the Chinese Exclusion Act of 1882. Extension was for an indefinite period of time.

1903—**Pensionado Act** allowed Filipino students to study in the U.S.

---

[1] **"mulattos"**—people with both white and black heritage.

1906—San Francisco school board demanded that all Asian students must attend segregated schools. Because of Japan's power, Japanese students were exempt from this decree.

1907—**The Immigration Act of 1907** reinforced and expanded restrictions on criminals and the insane, broadening the definitions of these categories. Section One of the act was aimed at keeping out Japanese and Koreans.

1907—**The Gentleman's Agreement** required Japan to impose restrictions on emigration to the United States in return for insuring the rights of Japanese already settled here. The agreement was reached to help relieve tensions developing between the U.S. and Japanese governments regarding the increasing number of national and state regulations on Japanese immigrants.

1913—**The California Alien Land Act** excluded aliens, mostly Japanese farmers, from owning land. Further restrictions were added in 1921 and 1923; later repealed in 1948.

1917—**The Immigration Act of 1917**, also called the **Barred Zone Act**, banned immigration from large geographical areas, mainly in Asia.

1921—**The Immigration Act of 1921** introduced a "quota system," or an annual limit on the number of immigrants from specific countries. Based on the 1910 census, nations were allowed an annual quota of 3% of that nationality's U.S. population. The intent of the law was to keep the ethnic mix of the country the same as it was in 1910.

1924—**The Immigration Act of 1924**, also called the **National Origins Act** or the **Johnson-Reed Act,** toughened the 1921 quota system by imposing a 2 percent rather than a 3 percent quota. It also based the quota on the 1890 census, a time before major waves of immigrants from eastern Europe had arrived. The intent was to restore an earlier heavily English and northern and western European, ethnic mix of the country.

The Laws from 1940–Present

1942—**Executive Order 9066** sanctioned the "relocation" of 110,000 Japanese Americans into ten U.S. internment camps.

1943—**Immigration Act of 1943**, also known as the **Magnuson Exclusion Act**, completely repealed the Chinese Exclusion Act of 1882, allowing Chinese immigrants to become naturalized citizens. However, only 105 Chinese a year were allowed to immigrate. The law reflects U.S. alliances with China during World War II.

1945—Internment camps were finally closed.

1946—**Bill of 1946**, also called the **Filipino Naturalization Act**, allowed people to immigrate from the Philippines and India. It also allowed Filipinos and Indians to become naturalized citizens. Quotas were set at 100 people per country per year.

1948—**Displaced Persons Act** allowed 3,500 Chinese, who were caught in the States because of the Chinese civil war, to remain in the United States. The Act granted them permanent resident status. California law banning interracial marriages was finally repealed after almost seventy years.

1952—**McCarran-Walter Act of 1952** removed all racial criteria for naturalization. Quotas were still small, but additional provisions allowed for the immigration of nonquota immigrants such as spouses and children. Communists, however, were barred.

1965—**The Nationality Act of 1965**, also called the **Hart Luce-Celler Act**, abolished the National Origins Act of 1924 quota system. It stated that family reunification would be the guiding principle for immigration.

1968—Cap of 12,000 was placed on immigrants from the western hemisphere. The number of Asian immigrants rose significantly.

1984—Filipino World War II veterans were denied U.S. citizenship even though they had fought for the United States.

1986—The **Immigration Reform and Control Act of 1986**, also called the **Simpson-Rodino Act**, raised the ceiling on immigration from Hong Kong from 600 to 5,000.

1988—**Civil Liberties Act of 1988** apologized to the thousands of Japanese Americans who were detained in internment camps during World War II.

1990—**Immigration Act of 1990** capped total immigration at 700,000 (lowered to 675,000 in 1995). Each nation was allowed 25,000 immigrants to the United States, not including refugees. Family reunification categories were retained. "Employment-creating" immigrants who were willing to invest $1 million in a U.S. concern were also allowed to immigrate. This action represented a clear class bias in that the rich could buy their way into the United States.

QUESTIONS TO CONSIDER

1. Why do you think the Chinese Exclusion Act and the Immigration Acts of 1921 and 1924 are among the most controversial legislation passed in United States history? What do you think the arguments for and against them would have been?

2. How do these laws reflect the perspectives provided in the two poems, "The New Colossus" and "Unguarded Gates"?

3. If you could write an Immigration Act for today, what would it be like?

Comprehensive Immigration Law

BY PRESIDENT CALVIN COOLIDGE

After the United States ventured into world politics in World War I (1914–1918), many people reacted by supporting "isolationism," a return to the traditional United States policy of avoiding alliances with other countries. Isolationism was reinforced by the negative reaction of native Americans to the large numbers of eastern and southern Europeans who immigrated between about 1880 and 1920 to fill jobs created by the Industrial Revolution. The famous "quota system" of the Immigration Acts of 1921 and 1924 allowed only a certain number of people to come from each country. The 1924 law's quotas were based on the ethnic composition of the United States in 1890. The law, which stayed in place until 1965, clearly favored immigrants from northern and western Europe.

Whereas it is provided in the act of Congress approved May 26, 1924, entitled "An act to limit the immigration of aliens into the United States, and for other purposes" that "The annual quota of any nationality shall be two per centum of the number of foreign-born individuals of such nationality resident in continental United States as determined by the United States Census of 1890, but the minimum quota of any nationality shall be 100 (Sec. 11 a). . . .

"The Secretary of State, the Secretary of Commerce, and the Secretary of Labor, jointly, shall, as soon as feasible after the enactment of this act, prepare a statement showing the number of individuals of the various nationalities resident in continental United States as determined by the United States Census of 1890, which statement shall be the population basis for the purposes of subdivision (a) of section 11 (Sec. 12 b).

"Such officials shall, jointly, report annually to the President the quota of each nationality under subdivision (a) of section 11, together with the statements, estimates, and revisions provided for in this section. The President shall proclaim and make known the quotas so reported." (Sec. 12 e)

Now, therefore I, Calvin Coolidge, President of the United States of America acting under and by virtue of the power invested in me by the aforesaid act of Congress, do hereby proclaim and make known that on and after July 1, 1924, and throughout the fiscal year 1924–1925, the quota of each nationality provided in said act shall be as follows:

COUNTRY OR AREA OF BIRTH QUOTA 1924–1925
Afghanistan—100 [individual immigrants]
Albania—100
Andorra—100
Arabian Peninsula—100
Armenia—124
Australia, including Papua, Tasmania, and all islands appertaining to Australia—21
Austria—785
Belgium—512
Bhutan—100

Bulgaria—100
Cameroon (proposed British mandate)—100
Cameroon (French mandate)—100
China—100
Czechoslovakia—3,073
Danzig, Free City of—228
Denmark—2,789
Egypt—100
Estonia—124
Ethiopia (Abyssinia)—100
Finland—170
France—3,954
Germany—51,227
Great Britain and Northern Ireland—34,007
Greece—100
Hungary—473
Iceland—100
India—100
Iraq (Mesopotamia)—100
Irish Free State—28,567
Italy, including Rhodes, Dodecanesia,
    and Castellorizzo—3,845
Japan—100
Latvia—142
Liberia—100
Liechtenstein—100
Lithuania—344
Luxemburg—100
Monaco—100
Morocco (French and Spanish Zones and Tangier)—100
Muscat (Oman)—100
Nauru (proposed British mandate)—100
Nepal—100
Netherlands—1,648
New Zealand (including appertaining islands)—100
Norway—6,453

New Guinea, and other Pacific Islands under proposed
    Australian mandate—100
Palestine (with Trans-Jordan, proposed British
    mandate)—100
Persia—100
Poland—5,982
Portugal—503
Rwanda and Urundi (Belgium mandate)—100
Rumania—603
Russia, European and Asiatic—2,248
Samoa, Western (proposed mandate of New
    Zealand)—100
San Marino—100
Siam—100
South Africa, Union of—100
South West Africa (proposed mandate of Union of
    South Africa)—100
Spain—131
Sweden—9,561
Switzerland—2,081
Syria and The Lebanon (French mandate)—100
Tanganyika (proposed British mandate)—100
Togoland (proposed British mandate)—100
Togoland (French mandate)—100
Turkey—100
Yap and other Pacific islands (under
    Japanese mandate)—100
Yugoslavia—671

GENERAL NOTE: The immigration quotas assigned to
the various countries and quota-areas should not be
regarded as having any political significance whatever,
or as involving recognition of new governments, or of
new boundaries, or of transfers of territory except as the
United States Government has already made such recognition in a formal and official manner.

QUESTIONS TO CONSIDER

1. What parts of the world are given the smallest quotas? The largest?

2. What message does this law give to countries with small quotas? With large quotas?

3. Does this legislation substantially change American policy toward countries of Asia? (You may want to look back at the previous legislation regarding restrictions on Asians.)

Roper Poll

COMMISSIONED BY NEGATIVE
POPULATION GROWTH

Most Americans today still think of the United States as a land of opportunity that welcomes all who seek a better life and who value freedom. However, many people worry that prosperity and stability cannot continue if controls are not placed on the large numbers of immigrants who want to come to this country every year. Immigration policy has been a major political issue during recent years, with the debate intensified by concerns about growing numbers of illegal immigrants from Latin America and refugees from Haiti, Cuba, Vietnam, and Eastern Europe. Negative Population Growth, Inc., a public interest group that favors tightening immigration restrictions, commissioned this opinion poll, conducted in 1995 by the Roper Organization, a well-known polling firm. The findings include the following:

Large and substantial margins agree that overall immigration should be lower. Eighty percent of all those interviewed favor a lower level of immigration than the current level of over one million a year. That share is mostly consistent among all segments of the population.

Most support less than 300,000 new immigrants a year. A large majority favor overall immigration at less than 300,000 per year. Seventy percent of all respondents support a level of immigration below 300,000 per year. This view is supported by 52 percent of Hispanics, 73 percent of Blacks, 72 percent of conservatives, 71 percent of moderates, 66 percent of liberals, 72 percent of Democrats, and 70 percent of Republicans.

Most want even larger cuts. A majority favors fewer than 100,000 overall new immigrants a year. A total of 54 percent say annual immigration should be less than 100,000. Twenty percent support no immigration at all—zero.

Trends correlate to income/education. Those most likely to face job competition from immigrants want the lowest levels of immigration possible. Higher than average support for zero immigration was expressed by those with less than a high school degree (29%) and those with household incomes below $15,000 (26%).

A large majority (75 percent) support strong laws to identify and deport illegal aliens. Only 10 percent disagree with strict laws against the removal of illegal aliens.

The strongest supporters of tough measures against illegal aliens are self-styled political moderates (78 percent), strongly religious (76 percent), whites (77 percent), Protestants (82 percent), and Midwesterners (85 percent). Support for tough laws against illegal aliens is supported by:

- 76% Democrats; 76% Republicans
- 75% Conservatives; 78% middle-of-the-roaders; 72% liberals
- 77% of whites; 68% of blacks; 60% of Hispanics (English-speaking)
- 69% of Catholics; 82% of Protestants; 54% of Jews; 71% other religions
- 84% Midwesterners; 74% Southerners; 74% Westerners; 63% New Englanders

- 76% non-high school grads; 73% high school grads; 76% some college; 73% college graduates

Most Americans also support population stabilization[1] by the year 2050. The majority (59 percent) would like to see our population no greater than today's population or smaller. Another 22 percent of the respondents would like to see our population stabilize somewhere between today's 265 million and the projected 400 million by 2050.

"The evidence is overwhelmingly clear," says Sharon McCloe Stein,[2] "it's time for Congress to cut immigration by two-thirds or more. This is an issue on which a national consensus has emerged: America is ready to cut back drastically on immigration," she said. NPG calls for Congress to pass, with strengthening amendments to reduce numbers further, comprehensive immigration bills now pending in Congress.

---

[1] population stabilization—no change in overall population.

[2] Sharon McCloe Stein—Washington director of Negative Population Growth (NPG), the group that commissioned this poll.

QUESTIONS TO CONSIDER

1. What groups of Americans are most likely to support tougher restrictions on immigration? Why?

2. Which of the following factors—ethnicity, party affiliation, religion, region, income level—seems *not* to be linked to significant differences in attitudes toward immigrants?

3. What is your opinion of the statement, "It's time for Congress to cut immigration by two-thirds or more"?

Organizing Labor

▲

Emma Goldman Anarchist and labor leader Emma Goldman was born in 1869 in a Jewish ghetto in Russia. She immigrated to America after refusing an arranged marriage at age fifteen. Working as a seamstress in Rochester, New York, Goldman found that conditions in America were in some ways worse than in Russia. After being jailed twice for various anarchist activities, she was stripped of her citizenship and deported in 1919.

Sweatshop Many immigrants found work in sweatshops. These people are making garments in a New York tenement.

▼

▲

Cesar Chavez Chavez (1927–1993) was one of the most influential Hispanic leaders in the Southwest in the twentieth century. He worked tirelessly on behalf of immigrant Mexican farm workers and he founded the National Farm Workers Association, which merged with another union to form the United Farm Workers. From 1965 to 1970, Chavez led a successful five-year nationwide boycott-strike against grape growers in California.

▲

Cotton Pickers On Strike Striking cotton pickers form a caravan near Tulare, California, in October 1933. The Great Depression worsened their already poor conditions, leading many groups to strike.

Grape Pickers At the heart of California's Imperial Valley agricultural industry are immigrant workers, like the grape pickers shown here in 1973.

▼

Americans Becoming More Tolerant

BY THE NATIONAL IMMIGRATION FORUM

Toward the end of the twentieth century laws increased restrictions on immigration. In 1995, for example, the total number of immigrants allowed per year was lowered to 675,000, down from 700,000 in 1990. The Immigration Act of 1996 made it easier to deport illegal aliens and toughened the penalties for smuggling aliens into the country. The results of the 1995 Roper Poll (see page 199) seemed to confirm that American political opinion supported a tough stance on immigration. To offset this perception, the National Immigration Forum posted on its web site the results of an August 1997 poll commissioned by USA Today and the Public Broadcasting System. Its findings are dramatically different from those of the Roper Poll and lead to questions regarding the path that legislation should take in the future. The poll, conducted by Princeton Survey Research, shows that American attitudes toward immigration are shifting. Americans are less threatened by today's level of immigration and are more comfortable with the diversity it brings. Here are some of the highlights.

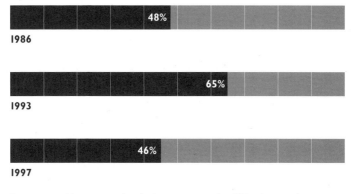

1986

1993

1997

Percentage of Americans who think immigration should be decreased or stopped.

Concern about Level of Immigration Drops Dramatically

The poll shows that Americans' concern about present levels of immigration has decreased dramatically in the last few years. The percentage of respondents who said that they thought immigration should be decreased or stopped was 46 percent. This compares to 65 percent in 1993. The percentage of respondents who felt that immigration should be kept at present levels or *increased* was 49 percent.

Confusion about How Immigrants Enter the Country May Exacerbate Perception of the Need to Reduce Immigration

The poll revealed that Americans are confused about legal vs. illegal immigration. Nearly 2/3 (64 percent) of respondents wrongly thought that more immigrants come into this country illegally than legally. It is possible that, if Americans better understood the way immigrants get here, they would be *even less* concerned about current levels of immigration. Three in four of those who think most immigrants arrive illegally say they want immigration reduced or stopped.

Greater Tolerance of Diversity

Americans are not as concerned as they were five years ago about the kind of immigrants who are coming in and how the racial composition of America is changing. Fifty-nine percent of respondents were either not concerned, or "not too concerned" that, as a result of the number and nationalities of immigrants coming into the country, whites of European descent will eventually lose their majority status. When asked how they feel about specific nationalities, only 45 percent of respondents felt that "too many" immigrants were entering the country from Latin America. This compares with 69 percent who thought so in 1992. Forty-one percent of respondents felt that "too many" immigrants were coming into the country from Asia. In 1992, 62 percent thought so.

Melting Pot: Still a Powerful Image

The idea of America as a melting pot of different cultures is still an important one for the majority of Americans. When asked, 55 percent of respondents said they felt that adapting and blending into the larger society is more important than maintaining distinct customs and traditions. Seventy-nine percent of respondents see the "blending of many different cultures into one" as a unique character of this country. The percentage who have this view is even higher among respondents who feel immigration should be kept at current levels or increased. Continued acceptance of immigrants may depend on how immigrants from many cultures continue to blend into our society. Evidence of this is the concern expressed by 44 percent of respondents who felt that the growing number and nationalities of immigrants will create "too much diversity" *in the future.*

Generational Differences

The poll revealed that younger and older respondents consistently differed in their responses. The younger generation, which has grown up in a diverse society, tends to be more tolerant of diversity. Older respondents were consistently more concerned about immigration and the diversity it is bringing. For example, concern about whites losing majority status was expressed by more than half (51 percent) of those over 65 years of age, but only by 32 percent of those 49 years or younger. Fifty-six percent of those 65 and older feel that the number and diverse nationalities of immigrants coming in will lead to "too much diversity" in the future. That concern dropped to 39 percent of those under age 50.

QUESTIONS FOR CONSIDERATION

1. What evidence does the poll provide for the conclusion that Americans are becoming more tolerant of immigrants and diversity?

2. How do attitudes toward America as a melting pot contradict or support the poll's conclusion that Americans are becoming more tolerant?

3. In what ways are the results of this poll different from those of the Roper Poll (p. 199). What might explain the differences?

Fair Treatment
for Refugees

BY THE NATIONAL IMMIGRATION FORUM

*Since American involvement in the Vietnam War (1965–1973), the
United States government has responded to an increasing demand
to loosen immigration restrictions for refugees from hot spots
around the world—places where civil war, persecution, and political
strife make it all but impossible for citizens to stay in their homes.
The United States government has allowed special asylum for
refugees from countries all over the world, including those from
war-ravaged Central America. When political upheavals in the
Caribbean nation of Haiti in 1991–94 drove immigrants to seek
refuge, many American leaders spoke out on their behalf. The
National Immigration Forum, a group that believes immigrants
have an important, positive role to play in American society, posted
an explanation, along with some of the leaders' statements, on its
web site. Congress reacted to the emergency by passing the Haitian
Refugee and Immigration Fairness Act of 1998, which allowed
Haitian nationals who had entered the United States to apply for
permanent residency.*

In 1997, Congress passed legislation to provide relief from deportation for some Central American, Cuban, and Eastern European immigrants whose status in the United States was called into question by overly restrictive provisions of the 1996 immigration law. The legislation, however, failed to include any form of assistance for Haitian refugees who also fled civil wars, persecution, and political strife in their homeland.

Disappointed and indignant at this clear **disparity**[1] of treatment based on nationality rather than circumstances, elected officials, religious leaders, and community representatives continue to **advocate**[2] for the fair treatment of Haitian refugees in America. On December 23, 1997, President Clinton used his executive authority to direct the Attorney General and the Immigration and Naturalization Service to defer the deportation of Haitian refugees for one year. In the meantime, "The Haitian Refugee and Immigration Fairness Act" has been introduced in both the House of Representatives and the Senate to provide permanent relief for these deserving refugees. On April 23rd, 1998, the bill was passed by the Senate Judiciary Committee and was later ratified in the Senate.

President Bill Clinton
Letter to Rep. Newt Gingrich (R-GA), Speaker of the House of Representatives, November 4, 1997

"I strongly urge the Congress to provide to Haitians treatment similar to that provided to Central Americans. In recent weeks, Members of Congress and representatives of the Haitian community have highlighted the compelling plight of thousands of Haitians in the United States. Their experiences parallel those of Central Americans in many ways. . . . These Haitians have made

---

[1] **disparity**—inequality.

[2] **advocate**—plead in favor of; urge; support.

vital contributions to their communities and have established deep roots in the United States. Providing them with an opportunity to gain permanent status in the U.S. is not only **equitable**,[3] but also critical to helping Haiti establish a strong and lasting democracy—a goal to which the United States continues to devote substantial energy and resources."

Sen. Spencer Abraham (R-MI), Chairman, Senate Subcommittee on Immigration

Statement, Senate Subcommittee on Immigration Hearing Concerning "The Haitian Refugee and Immigration Fairness Act," December 17, 1997

"U.S. immigration law should not turn on arbitrary distinctions between members of different nationalities. Rather it should treat like cases alike regardless of nationality."

Sen. Edward M. Kennedy (D-MA)

Statement, November 4, 1997

"Last year, Congress changed the rules and broke faith with thousands of refugee families from Central America and Haiti. These families fled civil war, death squads, and oppression. They found safe haven in America, and they have contributed significantly to the United States and to communities across the country."

Congressional Black Caucus

Letter signed by all 42 members of the Congressional Black Caucus, October 21, 1997

"Haitians have made vital contributions to their local communities in this country. Unfairly deporting them will tear apart many families who have abided by our laws."

---

[3] **equitable**—fair; just.

Rep. Xavier Becerra (D-CA), Chairman, The Congressional Hispanic Caucus
Press Release, November 4, 1997

"Our goal has been to treat all immigrants fairly and even-handedly. This latest legislation sets a dangerous precedent of favoring some while completely excluding others who find themselves in virtually identical circumstances. This is an issue of basic fairness."

Rep. Carrie P. Meek (D-FL)
"Treat Haitian Immigrants Fairly, Justly, Equally," Miami Herald, November 12, 1997

"In Miami, Nicaraguans, Salvadorans, Guatemalans, and Haitians live, work, worship, and raise their children side by side in our neighborhoods. If immigrants from different countries can do that in Miami, then surely our leaders from different political parties in Washington can put aside **partisan**[4] squabbling and treat Haitian immigrants fairly, justly, and equally."

Jack Kemp, former vice-presidential Republican candidate and former Secretary of Housing and Urban Development
Letter to Speaker Newt Gingrich, February 24, 1998

"The Haitians are in the same bind as the Central Americans whom Congress helped last year: they face a threat of deportation after years in this country. The number of Haitians is far smaller than the number of Central Americans and their individual cases are equally, if not more, compelling. They have all presented cases for asylum or refugee status, and about a third cleared the first hurdle when they were interviewed in Guantanamo by INS[5] agents and were able to establish

---

[4] **partisan**—relating to support for the different political parties in Congress.

[5] INS—Immigration and Naturalization Service, the major agency charged with implementing U.S. immigration policy. The immigrants were held at the American naval base in Guantanamo Bay until the INS could determine if they were legitimate refugees, not, for instance, criminals or others who would not meet immigration standards for admission to the United States.

a credible fear of persecution. Like the Central Americans, they have put down roots here, their families are growing up here, and their communities have welcomed them. . . . in my mind this issue presents a chance to do the right thing by **rectifying**[6] an omission in last year's bill, and to uphold our nation's tradition of accepting refugees."

Catholic Bishops of Florida
Statement published in the Miami Herald, *June 18, 1998*
"The Plight of the Haitian community in Florida has always been of special concern to the Roman Catholic bishops of Florida. We pray that [Congress] will act to right the injustice done to those who fled their island home, suffering from persecution, to seek safety and protection in the United States. . . . It will be sad for our state and tragic for these people if Congress does not act to remedy the injustice that exists in singling out Haitians."

Grover Joseph Rees, former General Counsel, U.S. Immigration and Naturalization Service
Testimony, Senate Subcommittee on Immigration Hearing Concerning "The Haitian Refugee and Immigration Fairness Act," December 17, 1997
"Haitians who were paroled into the United States between 1991 and 1994 . . . came at a time when their country was being ruled by a particularly brutal regime. . . . Moreover, like many of the groups who benefited from prior legislation, these people have built their lives here in the United States."

---

[6] **rectifying**—correcting; making right.

Amnesty International[7]

Testimony, Senate Subcommittee on Immigration Hearing Concerning "The Haitian Refugee and Immigration Fairness Act," December 17, 1997

"Amnesty International's conclusion is that anyone returning to Haiti cannot be assured that they will be protected by the existing Haitian justice system from former officials who occasioned their flight. Given the concerns raised above, such assurances would appear to fall far short of what would guarantee safe return. Any blanket assessment that the change in government can allow all who fled the country to return without fear or harm is therefore incorrect in our view."

---

[7] **Amnesty International**—organization whose major goal is to identify and support people in need of refuge in countries around the world.

QUESTIONS TO CONSIDER

1. What argument does the article make for an immigration policy based on circumstances, rather than on nationality? What is your opinion of this argument?

2. What arguments do various officials give for allowing Haitian refugees to stay in the United States?

3. What arguments do you think people who opposed this law might have made against it?

Latino America

BY BROOK LARMER

During most of the twentieth century, Latino immigrants came to the United States to take low-paying jobs with little security, such as migrant farming and sweatshop labor. By the end of the century, Latinos had transformed their image and influence. According to journalist Brook Larmer, in the July 12, 1999, issue of Newsweek International, Latino political and cultural impact was becoming enormous.

Hispanics are hip, hot, and making history. By 2005, Latinos will be the largest U.S. minority; they're already shaping pop culture and presidential politics. The Latin wave will change how the country looks—and how it looks at itself.

Strolling along northwest Eighth Street in Miami—a.k.a.[1] Calle Ocho—is like taking a trip through another country. But last week the sights and sounds of Calle Ocho were both intensely foreign and undeniably American. A crowd of angry Cuban exiles marched

---

[1] a.k.a.—also known as.

down the street denouncing the U.S. Coast Guard's use of force to round up six Cuban refugees near a local beach the day before. From the sidelines, other Latinos looked on: prim Honduran clerks at an evangelical bookstore, spiffed-up businessmen at an Argentine steakhouse, sweaty construction workers eating Salvadoran *pupusas*.[2] *Merengue*[3] music blasted indifferently from the Do-Re-Mi music shop. But the elderly Cubans playing dominoes in Maximo Gomez Park stood and joined in with the protesters: "Libertad! Libertad!"

Could this be the face of America's future? Better believe it. No place in the United States is quite so international as Miami; even the Latinos who run the city joke that they like it "because it's so close to America." But Miami, like New York and Los Angeles, is ground zero for a **demographic**[4] upheaval that is unfolding across America. Like the arrival of European immigrants at the turn of the century, the tide of Hispanic immigrants—and the fast growth of Latino families—has injected a new energy into the nation's cities.

Latinos are changing the way the country looks, feels and thinks, eats, dances, and votes. From teeming immigrant **meccas**[5] to small-town America, they are filling churches, building businesses and celebrating their Latin heritage. In a special *Newsweek* Poll of Latinos, 83 percent said being Hispanic was important to their identity. They are overwhelmingly Roman Catholic; 42 percent go to church once a week. They've become a **potent**,[6] increasingly unpredictable political force: 37 percent of 18- to 34-year-old Latinos say they are independent, about twice as many as their Hispanic elders. In

---

[2] *pupusas*—hand-held fried snacks.

[3] *Merengue*—lively, distinctly Latin music.

[4] **demographic**—distribution of population by factors like race, age, gender, ethnic group, and the like.

[5] **meccas**—desirable destinations; named after Mecca, a city in Saudi Arabia, where millions of Muslims flock for an annual religious pilgrimage.

[6] **potent**—powerful.

America, a country that constantly redefines itself, the rise of Latinos also raises questions about race, identity and culture—and whether the United States will ever truly be one nation.

The numbers couldn't be clearer. Fueled by massive (and mostly legal) immigration and high birthrates, the Latino population has grown 38 percent since 1990—to 31 million—while the overall population has grown just 9 percent. And with more than a third of the Latino population still under 18, the boom is just beginning. By the year 2005, Latinos are projected to be the largest minority in the country, passing non-Hispanic blacks for the first time. By 2050, nearly one quarter of the population will be Latino. "The [African-American] civil-rights slogan was 'We shall overcome,'" says Christy Haubegger, the 30-year-old founding editor of the bilingual magazine *Latina*. "Ours is going to be 'We shall overwhelm.'"

They may just have the muscle to back that up—particularly in politics. Though they accounted for only 6 percent of those who voted in the 1998 midterm elections, Hispanics are clustered in 11 key states, with a total of 217 out of the 270 Electoral College votes needed for the presidency. And neither party has a lock on this new force. "Latinos are the soccer moms[7] of the year 2000," says Gregory Rodriguez of the New America Foundation. Is it any wonder that Al Gore and George W. Bush were both on campaign stops in Florida and California last week, eagerly greeting voters in Spanish?

The driving force behind the Latino wave are members of a **cohort**[8] that is sometimes called Generation Ñ.[9] These young Hispanics—the Latin Gen X[10]—are influential

---

[7] soccer moms—young mothers noted for their voting power during recent presidential elections.

[8] **cohort**—group.

[9] The letter *n* with a tilde (~) over it is used in Spanish to indicate the pronunciation (ny). The designation "Generation Ñ," therefore, acknowledges it is a group of Spanish-speaking people.

[10] Gen X—Generation X, referring to Americans born during the late 1960s and 1970s.

not simply because of their huge numbers. They are making their mark—and making all things Latin suddenly seem cool. Jose Canseco, a 35-year-old Cuban-American, and Dominican-born Sammy Sosa, 30, lead the great American home-run derby. Ricky Martin, 27, and Jennifer Lopez, 28, top the pop-music charts. Actors Benjamin Bratt, 35, and Salma Hayek, 30, are quickening the national pulse.

Is the rest of America ready? Hip Anglos on both coasts are dancing salsa, learning Spanish and dabbling in Nuevo Latino cuisine. And every fifth grader seems to know the lyrics of "Livin' La Vida Loca." But many Latinos doubt whether America can easily move past the stereotypes that depict them as illegals, gangbangers or entertainers. "Don't try to understand Latinos through [Ricky Martin]," says Manuel Magana, 21, a University of Michigan senior. "It's like trying to figure out Americans by listening to the Backstreet Boys."

Latinos can't be neatly **pigeonholed**.[11] They come from 22 different countries of origin, including every hybrid possible. Many are white, some are black, but most are somewhere in between. Some Latino families have been in the United States for centuries, since the days when much of the Southwest was still a part of Mexico. Others, like the six Cuban refugees, swam ashore last week. (The Coast Guard freed them a day later.) Many Latinos are **assimilating**[12] into cycles of urban blight; 40 percent of Latino children now live in poverty, the highest rate ever. But millions of Hispanics are also moving into the middle class, speaking English, inter-marrying and spending cash—lots of it. U.S. Latinos pump $300 billion a year into the economy.

---

[11] **pigeonholed**—classified.

[12] **assimilating**—becoming absorbed.

Not everybody has been eager to give Latinos a big *abrazo*.[13] When California voters passed propositions limiting immigrant rights and Washington tightened federal immigration policy in the mid-1990s, Latinos took it as a call to arms. The best weapons of defense were citizenship and the vote. Between 1994 and 1998, Latino voting in nationwide midterm elections jumped 27 percent even as overall voter turnout dropped 13 percent. The 2000 presidential election may show even more dramatic increases: Latino leaders aim to register an additional 3 million voters by then.

Latinos have long leaned Democratic (Clinton got 72 percent), but their vote is alluring these days precisely because it is up for grabs—and Generation Ñ seems intent on keeping it that way. Gore edged out Bush among all Latinos polled, 29 percent to 28 percent, but Generation Ñ voters favored Bush by a margin of 9 percent. Nobody understands how Latinos can swing an election more than Nevada Sen. Harry Reid, a Democrat. During his tight 1998 race, Reid's friend, boxing promoter Bob Arum, persuaded Oscar De La Hoya to join the campaign. The **charismatic**[14] boxer did two fund-raisers, a public rally and several Spanish media spots. "He's the reason I'm in the Senate now," says Reid. Don't believe him? The senator won by just 428 votes.

Latinos are flattered to be considered hot commodities, whether as voters, consumers, employees or entertainers. But their aspirations, and their importance to American society, run much deeper than mere social acceptance. They are not "crossing-over" into mainstream America; they are already here, getting more influential by the day, so the rest of America must learn to adapt as well. "Something tremendous is happening,"

---

[13] *abrazo*—embrace, hug.

[14] **charismatic**—personally magnetic, charming.

says 30-year-old novelist Ixta Maya Murray. "This generation of Latinos is going to change the way America looks at itself." On the last Independence Day of the millennium, a new nation is being born.

—*With Veronica Chambers, Ana Figueroa, Pat Wingert and Julie Weingarten*, Newsweek International, *July 12, 1999.*

QUESTIONS TO CONSIDER

1. What was meant by the comment regarding a possible slogan for Latino rights: "We shall overwhelm"?

2. In what ways does the younger generation (Generation Ñ) of Latinos appear to be different from older generations?

3. In what ways have Latinos already changed American life? How might they influence it in the future?

La Migra

BY PAT MORA

The long border between Mexico and the United States has been a source of conflict between the two nations for many years. Because the border follows few natural obstructions it is easily crossed, making trade and immigration difficult for both countries to regulate. The United States maintains a Border Patrol to catch and deport illegal immigrants from Mexico who are attracted to better-paying jobs and to relatives already living across the border. This poem by Pat Mora describes the attitude of many Mexican Americans toward the patrol agents and challenges the job that they do.

I

Let's play *La Migra*[1]
I'll be the Border Patrol.
You be the Mexican maid.
I get the badge and sunglasses.
You can hide and run,

---

[1] *La Migra*—term used by Mexican Americans along the border for the patrol agents.

but you can't get away
because I have a jeep.
I can take you wherever
I want, but don't ask
questions because
I don't speak Spanish.
I can touch you wherever
I want but don't complain
too much because I've got
boots and kick—if I have to,
and I have handcuffs.
Oh, and a gun.
Get ready, get set, run.

II

Let's play *La Migra*
You be the Border Patrol.
I'll be the Mexican woman.
Your jeep has a flat,
and you have been spotted
by the sun.
All you have is heavy: hat,
glasses, badge, shoes, gun.
I know this desert,
where to rest,
where to drink.
Oh, I am not alone.
You hear us singing
and laughing with the wind,
Agua dulce brota aquí,
aquí, aquí,[2] but since you
can't speak Spanish
you do not understand.
Get ready.

---

[2] *Agua dulce brota aquí, aquí, aquí*—Sweet water flows here, here, here.

QUESTIONS TO CONSIDER

1. What attitudes are reflected in this poem?

2. What advantages does the Border Patrol have over the Mexican immigrant?

3. What skills do immigrants have that the agents don't?

4. What does the poet mean by her last phrase, "Get ready"?

5. What is your opinion of the United States maintaining a Border Patrol?

Recasting the Melting Pot

BY ROBERTO SURO

Traditionally throughout American history, the process that immigrants experience as they adjust to their new life has been described as a "melting pot." Immigrants must change their habits and beliefs in order to survive, and gradually over the course of two or three generations their differences disappear. They become assimilated, or absorbed, into American culture. Even though the melting pot theory allows that large numbers and varieties of immigrants may change the general culture, the implication is that the immigrant's original identity is lost. In this 1999 essay for American Demographics *magazine, Roberto Suro argues that the melting pot theory does not apply to Latino immigrants of the second half of the twentieth century.*

Becoming an American used to be simple, or at least that's the way we conjure up the old Ellis Island days of immigration. Foreigners happily left the old country behind and steadily assumed a new identity. Peddler, Plumber, Professional. Little Italy, Brooklyn, Long

Island. The predictable transition was complete by the time the newcomers' grandchildren grew up—speaking just a few words in the mother tongue and practicing an ethnic identity attached to holidays rather than everyday life. It didn't happen exactly that way for a lot of families during the first half of the 20th century, but nonetheless the myth of the melting pot informs our expectations for the first half of the next century, when another great wave of immigrants will be finding its place here.

Nearly half of all immigrants today—legal and illegal—come from Spanish-speaking countries. Based on their high birth rates, the U.S. Census Bureau predicts that native and foreign-born Latinos will account for more than 40 percent of U.S. population growth in the next decade, compared to less than 25 percent for non-Hispanic whites. Unfortunately, the melting pot metaphor does not help much in understanding where this demographic change is taking the nation. Indeed, despite the centrality of this myth in the American consciousness, it may create false or dangerously misleading expectations as far as Latinos are concerned, especially the second generation—the children of immigrants—who undergo the most profound change.

Fortunately, even though we are still at the front end of the assimilation process, some major signposts are available. Look at occupations and education, listen to the music, eavesdrop at dinner table conversations, and you do not see a singular, straight-line progression toward some American norm. Second-generation Latinos are indeed adopting new identities, but they set off in a lot of different directions and, in many cases, the results differ from the linear progression that mainstream America expects based on its idealized memory of the past.

Consider banda music, an innovative mix of rock, salsa, country-western, and norte-o—the traditional folk music of northern Mexico. Banda originated with groups that regularly toured the U.S. and Mexico, picking up bits of music in both countries. Precisely because it is so **eclectic**,[1] banda became a huge fad in Southern California in the 1990s.

All-banda radio stations rocketed to huge audience ratings by attracting Latinos of all sorts, including both newly arrived immigrants and those whose ancestry in Los Angeles dates back several generations. Kids who were deeply into hip-hop turned in their basketball shoes and baseball caps for boots and cowboy hats, then headed for night clubs, where they spun around in elaborately **choreographed**[2] steps.

The music, the dress, and the dancing are neither Mexican nor American, but rather a constantly evolving mixture of the two. Banda is the anthem of a transnational space that is not only home to newcomers and the native born, but also serves as a way-station for Latinos who easily travel between neighboring nations.

Of course, a strong homeland influence has been typical of many immigrant communities throughout history. But Latino immigration is unique in the American experience because it comes from countries so nearby. Many Dominican entrepreneurs run bodegas (neighborhood grocery stores) in both New York City and Santo Domingo, shipping merchandise and capital back and forth and working in both places as it suits them. Farm hands from central Mexico readily come north for the summer home-construction season in the United States and still remain fully productive participants in the work of the family rancho. And now, with the end of civil strife in their homelands, long-term residents from Central America can cut the emotional costs of migration by visiting their families for the Christmas holidays, to attend a wedding, or to sit out a spell of unemployment here.

---

[1] **eclectic**—varied.

[2] **choreographed**—designed, as for a dance.

Banda music is just one example of how this steady, often circular human flow constantly refreshes the sounds of Spanish in Latino communities and even reawakens ethnic identity among English-speaking Latinos. At the very least, this easy access to the homeland allows many Latinos to prolong a **sojourner**[3] mentality and put off coming to terms with the American realities. Many Latinos come to the United States expecting to stay just long enough to earn a little pile of money, but end up making a life of it once they have children here. **Proximity**[4] also means that assimilation is not continuous or direct, but rather a rhythmic, periodic process in which immigrants retain aspects of their foreign identity even as they learn English and otherwise adopt American ways.

According to the melting pot myth, Americanization and economic progress go hand-in-hand. As an individual or a family rises toward the middle class, ethnic identification is supposed to diminish; meanwhile, foreign traits remain most pronounced among the poor. The most economically successful Latino immigrants, however—the Cubans in South Florida—have resolutely retained a Latino identity and Spanish as a favored language.

Granted, Cubans are an exceptional case, but there are enough exceptions among Latino immigrants to disprove the rule. Minority group politics and civil rights policies, for example, produce a greater sense of ethnic identification among Latinos who are taking the first steps toward economic advancement than among those who are left behind. It is young people going to college or graduate school or applying for white-collar jobs who are most aware of affirmative action[5] and therefore have the most to gain by formally identifying themselves as a member of a minority group.

---

[3] **sojourner**—traveler.

[4] **Proximity**—geographic closeness.

[5] affirmative action—programs sponsored by the federal government to promote equal rights for minority groups.

European immigrants understood exclusion in terms of their "otherness"—their accents, religions, and the surnames they brought with them. For Latinos, an understanding of minority group status comes only after enough assimilation to perceive historical grievances[6] against the white majority and to acquire hyphenation—that is to move from being Mexican to becoming Mexican-American.

Assessing assimilation among Latino immigrants and their offspring who remain poor is the most urgent and difficult task of all. Should young, second-generation Latinos be considered successfully assimilated when they form street gangs, mark territories with spray-painted tags, deal in crack-cocaine, engage in car-jackings, and punish their enemies with drive-by shootings? Those are, after all, American-made behaviors learned here, and they mark a form of adaptation to American realities. Recently, in a **morbid**[7] variation on transnationalism, several U.S. street gangs have established branches in El Salvador through the missionary work of youths deported after committing violent crimes here.

More worrisome are the rising rates of high-school dropouts and teen pregnancies among Latinos, especially foreign-born youths, even as the same rates decline for whites and blacks. One big problem is the number of immigrant youths who go straight to work and never enroll in school here. But authoritative studies also indicate that among those who do enter U.S. schools, achievement levels tend to decline after a few years and homework effort drops as immigrant youth begin to spend the same amount of time in front of the television set as their native-born counterparts.

---

[6] historical grievances—mistreatments in the past.

[7] **morbid**—diseased; unwholesome; unhealthy.

By contrast, assimilation meant academic advancement for the children of European immigrants. Looking back at how the second- and third-generation Europeans became Americans, it's easy to forget that a series of extraordinary events forged a new and powerful national identity during the middle decades of this century: the shared adversity of the Great Depression, World War II, and the Cold War; the rising tide of the industrial economy; and the massive public-sector investments in **upward mobility**[8] by way of the G.I. Bill and the expansion of state university systems. All of that produced the heat that helped melt ethnics into a somewhat homogeneous middle class.

Absent such factors now, the offspring of today's immigrants are likely to follow more varied and complex paths. Many Latinos undoubtedly will pursue and achieve the prototypical American Dream in the suburbs. Yet even as they conform in some ways, other aspects of their identity—musical tastes or business arrangements, perhaps—will remain linked to homeland realities. Others may model themselves after native-born Latinos whose identity derives from the minority-group experience. A large number will absorb the distinct culture of American urban poverty. Given the multiple outcomes already in evidence, it is important not to base expectations on an idealized past, but instead to understand that during a time of immigration, change comes to both the newcomers and the hosts.

---

[8] **upward mobility**—improvement of social and economic conditions.

QUESTIONS TO CONSIDER

1. In what ways does the geographic closeness of relatives in their homelands affect the assimilation of Latinos into American life?

2. What evidence does the author provide to support his belief that the melting pot theory does not apply to recent Latino immigrants?

3. What historical factors make assimilation in the second half of the twentieth century different from that in the first half?

4. According to the author, what new immigration patterns may be emerging today?

Successful Integration of Immigrants

BY THE NATIONAL IMMIGRATION FORUM

Immigration has taken many different shapes and forms during American history. In the United States of the late eighteenth century, most immigrants came from a few countries of northern and western Europe. As the country expanded westward and new lands opened for settlement, immigrants from many other areas of the world came to escape hardships in their homelands and to seek their fortunes in America. Despite the many different groups arriving over hundreds of years, the immigrant experience has been in many ways the same. Immigrants have had to strike a balance between the challenges of assimilation and the need to retain their identities. Somehow they have always managed to do just that. This recent study of American immigrants confirms that the pattern continues successfully today, just as it has throughout the history of the United States.

Background

Anyone subjected to the intellectual debates on immigration of the past twenty years might easily conclude that immigrant assimilation is a thing of the past. At one extreme, right-wing nativists[1] fear a collapse of the nation's common culture, asserting that today's immigrants are unwilling to become part and parcel of the nation's social fabric. At the other end of the spectrum, left-wing academic multiculturalists[2] argue that today's immigrants should not be expected to assimilate into the culture they themselves have absorbed.

Fortunately, most immigrants do not conduct their lives according to the trends of café society.[3] Contemporary immigrant families overwhelmingly do what newcomers have always done: slowly, often painfully, but quite assuredly, embrace the cultural norms that are part of life in the United States.

Assimilation into life in the U.S. has never required the **obliteration**[4] of ethnic identity. Instead, it involves newcomers of differing backgrounds adopting basic concepts of American life—equality under the law, due process, and economic opportunity. Put another way, assimilation is not about immigrants rejecting their past, but about people of different racial, religious, and cultural backgrounds coming to believe that they are part of an overarching American family.

Assimilation is not now, and has never been, an instant transformation in which an immigrant suddenly becomes a "full-fledged American." Rather, it is a long-term, sometimes multigenerational, process. To some

---

[1] right-wing nativists—politically conservative people who want to preserve the "native" culture and keep new immigrants out.

[2] left-wing academic multiculturalists—politically liberal, university people who defend the right of individuals to retain their culture and resist assimilation.

[3] café society—fashionable people who make idle conversation on matters that don't directly affect them.

[4] **obliteration**—destruction; removal of all characteristics.

extent, it is never-ending: almost all Americans carry some of their ethnic past with them. Furthermore, U.S. culture constantly changes and adapts to immigrants, just as immigrants adapt to it. The nation remains, in the words of sociologist Nathan Glazer, "the permanently unfinished country."

Methodology

This study focuses on four areas that we consider **indices**[5] of an immigrant's commitment to American society—citizenship, homeownership, English language acquisition, and intermarriage. In assessing these four quantifiable indices of assimilation, we have chosen to rely on the 1990 U.S. census. Although conducted nine years ago, the decennial census is still the most reliable source of data on these indices. It is based on a large sample, which allows us to extract data on individual immigrant groups with great confidence. For intermarriage data, we also use the June 1994 Current Population Survey, which tracks generational differences. For the most recent totals of the numbers of immigrants and where they reside in the United States, we rely exclusively on the 1998 Current Population Survey.

Overview of Findings

Citizenship

In 1990, more than three-quarters (76.4 percent) of immigrants who had resided in the U.S. for forty years were naturalized.

Citizenship is the most symbolic sign of attachment to the United States. Whereas immigration itself can be reactive—a response to pressures in the home country—becoming a citizen is **quintessentially**[6] proactive. Not

---

[5] **indices**—measurements.

[6] **quintessentially**—purely; most essentially.

surprisingly, studies have shown that naturalized citizens tend to have a positive outlook on the United States. Once naturalized, immigrants also take on a more active role in the civic life of the country.

The longer immigrants reside in the United States, the more likely they are to become U.S. citizens. While rates vary among different groups, in 1990 three-quarters (76.4 percent) of immigrants who had resided in the U.S. for forty years were naturalized. In the past few years, political conditions in the United States have effected a change in attitudes toward naturalization. The anti-immigrant campaigns in California and in Congress in the middle and late 1990s[7] have been partly responsible for the largest rush to naturalization in the history of the United States.

Homeownership

Within twenty years of arrival in the U.S., well over half (60.9 percent) of immigrants lived in owner-occupied housing in 1990.

Homeownership is perhaps the most visible and durable sign that immigrants have set down roots in the United States. For most Americans—both native and foreign-born—buying a house is the principal means of accumulating wealth. There is no greater symbol of stability, permanence, and faith in the future.

Immigrants are making significant strides toward homeownership. Within twenty years of arrival in the United States, six out of ten immigrants lived in owner-occupied housing in 1990. In thirteen of the fifteen most populous immigrant groups, two out of three households were owner-occupied after twenty-six years of residence in the United States.

---

[7] This is a reference to anti-immigrant activities that sought to place new restrictions on immigration rates, to deny government services for noncitizens, and to set new requirements for residency.

English Language Acquisition

Within ten years of arriving in the U.S., more than three out of four immigrants spoke English well or very well in 1990. Less than 2 percent of long-established, forty-year-plus immigrants spoke no English at all.

Immigrants are much better prepared in English than is commonly thought. In 1990, a majority (58.2 percent) of immigrants who had arrived in the previous five years reported that they already spoke English "well" or "very well." Within ten years of arrival, a little more than three-quarters (76.3 percent) of immigrants spoke English with high proficiency. Only 1.7 percent of long-established immigrants reported speaking no English at all in 1990.

Taking a look at the second and third generations, virtually all children of immigrants spoke English proficiently. In most cases, the native language of immigrants is completely lost after a few generations in the United States. In 1990, 98.3 percent of Asian-American children reported speaking English "well," "very well," or exclusively, and 95.7 percent of third-generation Latino children spoke English "well," "very well," or exclusively. The idea of non-English speaking clusters remaining over generations is simply untrue. Sociologists have even designated the United States a "language graveyard."

Intermarriage

Intermarriage rates for second- and third-generation Asians and Latinos are extraordinarily high.

Intermarriage is not only a sign that a person has **transcended**[8] the ethnic segregation—both coerced and self-imposed—of the first years of immigration, it is also the most potent example of how Americans forge a common national experience out of a diverse cultural past. Intermarried couples and their children are living testaments to the fundamental tolerance underpinning a

---

[8] **transcended**—risen above; overpassed; exceeded.

multi-ethnic society. Clearly, intermarriage illustrates the extent to which ethnicity no longer serves to separate one American from another.

Both foreign-born Asians and foreign-born Hispanics have higher rates of intermarriage than do U.S.-born whites and blacks. By the third generation, intermarriage rates for Asians and Latinos, the two largest ethnic groups among contemporary immigrants, are extremely high. Fully one-third of third-generation Hispanic women are married to non-Hispanics, and 41 percent of third-generation Asian-American women have non-Asian spouses.

Conclusion

All available evidence shows that today's immigrants assimilate into U.S. society much the way earlier waves of newcomers did. The proof exists not in the rhetoric of the heated battles over immigration, but in the data revealing the often overlooked, everyday lives of contemporary immigrants and their families.

QUESTIONS TO CONSIDER

1. According to the researchers, what do rates of citizenship, home ownership, English language acquisition, and intermarriage indicate about immigrants?

2. Explain why sociologists have labeled the United States a "language graveyard."

3. How do intermarriage rates compare to rates for English language acquisition, home ownership, and citizenship? What do you think explains the differences?

4. What attitudes did the National Immigration Forum hope to change by publishing this study? Explain your answer with information from the text.

ACKNOWLEDGEMENTS

Texts

41 Reprinted with the permission of Simon & Schuster from *The Kennedy's* by Peter Collier and David Horowitz. Copyright © 1984 by Peter Collier and David Horowitz.

48 From "Life in New York Tenement Houses" in *Gaslight New York Revisited*, edited by Frank Oppel. Copyright © 1989 by Castle Books, a division of Book Sales, Inc. Used by permission of the publisher.

87 "California Zoot Suit War" from *Time* Magazine, June 21, 1943. Copyright © 1943 Time Inc. Reprinted by permission.

92 "Life As An Alien" by Meri Nana-Ama Danquah. Copyright © by 1998 Meri Nana-Ama Danquah. Reprinted by permission of Meri Nana-Ama Danquah and the Watkins/Loomis Agency.

105 From "Address by Cesar Chavez, President United Farm Workers of America, to AFL-CIO," The Commonwealth Club of California. San Francisco, November 9, 1984. Reprinted by permission.

139 "Choosing a Dream: Italians in Hell's Kitchen" by Mario Puzo, from *The Immigrant Experience* by Thomas C. Wheeler. Copyright © 1971 by Doubleday, a division of Bantam Doubleday Dell Publishing Group, Inc. Used by permission of Doubleday, a division of Random House, Inc.

157 "Old Country Advice to the American Traveler" from *My Name Is Aram*, copyright 1939 and renewed 1967 by William Saroyan, reprinted by permission of Harcourt, Inc.

162 From "The Rather Difficult Case of Mr. K*A*P*L*A*N" from *The Education of Hyman Kaplan* by Leonard Ross, copyright 1937 by Harcourt, Inc. and renewed 1965 by Leo C. Rosten, reprinted by permission of the publisher.

170 From "California Palms" by lê thi diem thúy, from *Half and Half: Writers on Growing Up Biracial and Bicultural* (Pantheon). Copyright © 1998 by lê thi diem thúy. Reprinted by permission of lê thi diem thúy and the Watkins/Loomis Agency.

199 From "U.S. Border Control" website: http://usbc.org/surveys/npg-poll.htm.

206 From "New Poll Shows Americans Becoming More Tolerant of Immigrants, Diversity" (no author) from The National Immigration Forum, http://www.immigrationforum.org/USATodayPol.html (February 7, 2000). Reprinted by permission.

210 From "Leaders Call for Fair Treatment of Haitian Refugees" (no author) from The National Immigration Forum, http://www.immigrationforum.org/archiveissues/haitians/leaders_call.html., (February 7, 2000). Reprinted by permission.

216 "Latino America" by Brook Larmer from *Newsweek*, July 12, 1999. Copyright © 1999 Newsweek, Inc. All rights reserved. Reprinted by permission.

222 "La Migra" from *Agua Santa/Holy Water* by Pat Mora. Copyright © 1995 by Pat Mora. Reprinted by permission of Beacon Press, Boston.

225 "Recasting the Melting Pot" by Roberto Suro. Reprinted from *American Demographics* magazine, March, 1999. Courtesy of Intertec Publishing Corp., Stamford, Connecticut. All Rights Reserved.

232 "From Newcomers to New Americans: The Successful Integration of Immigrants Executive Summary "(no author), http://www.immigrationforum.org/fromnewcomers.htm. (February 7, 2000.) Reprinted by permission.

Images

Photo Research Diane Hamilton

30–36, 58–62, 128–133, 186–188, 202–205 Courtesy Library of Congress.

Every effort has been made to secure complete rights and permissions for each selection presented herein. Updated acknowledgements, if needed, will appear in subsequent printings.

Index